Francis A. (Francis Allen) Horton

A Pastoral Journey

Being some Account of the Experience of the Rev. Francis A. Horton

Francis A. (Francis Allen) Horton

A Pastoral Journey
Being some Account of the Experience of the Rev. Francis A. Horton

ISBN/EAN: 9783744746120

Printed in Europe, USA, Canada, Australia, Japan

Cover: Foto ©Lupo / pixelio.de

More available books at **www.hansebooks.com**

Being Some Account of the Experiences of the Rev. Francis A. Horton as a Delegate to the Pan-Presbyterian Council.

BY THE

REV. FRANCIS A. HORTON

Pastor of the First Presbyterian Church, of Oakland, Cal.

———

OAKLAND, CAL:
TRIBUNE PUBLISHING COMPANY, 413, 415 AND 417 EIGHTH STREET.
1889.

PREFACE.

KIND Friends, who may dip into these letters here and there, or who may read them page by page, you will spare them your more severe tests when you recall the fact that they were written on the wing, and that since our return the cares of a heavy church have stood in the way of any recast, beyond a stray word or sentence or incident to make our thought clear or to correct errors in the first print. We had no idea but that the birth and burial of each letter would occur in the same issue of *The Tribune*. Still it is very grateful to us to find that the child born for a day is desired for a longer life. This wish could not well have been met but for the enterprise of the proprietors of *The Tribune*, who kindly undertake it at their own expense, solely to gratify their many friends and patrons who have expressed the wish both to them and to us.

If our fireside chat may yield a pleasant hour or two now and then, if it may inspire hard working men to take pity on themselves before friends need to pity their poor widows, if it may broaden any one's idea of living, if it may bring any back home, made over in brain and brawn, set back five or ten years towards youth in point of health and vigor, we shall be very happy, and in the hope that some such issues may come from this venture,

I remain, sincerely,

FRANCIS A. HORTON.

Oakland, January, 1889.

A PASTORAL JOURNEY.

Oakland is home to wife and me, and no mistake. " 'Tis home where'er the heart is," whether among glistening peaks or on blistering sands. How much to be envied are they whose hearts are set upon our beautiful city on the bay unequaled, and who find therein their home. The many tender words spoken and written to us in the past few days as well as previously, the hearty send off, blending with memories of five years of hard work crowned with a fair measure of success, fill our minds as the wheels are ever rolling us away, away. The glories of nature revealed in Oakland, the beauties of the town, the sentiments of loving hearts, all unite in one presence and impression. Fact is, wife and I are downright homesick to-night and would give a handsome sum if the round of duty and recreation were traversed and we were this near to home again. After all, what is there in life but love? Love is the constraining power, the inspiring genius. Love that reaches upward and impels to pureness and nobility, love that reaches into the home and directs labors and sacrifices for others' comfort, love that goes out to all and purifies society for the moral health of all.

> " What a world this might be
> If men were true and kind."

Now that the harness is really off, reaction sets in. Headache prevails, accompanied by general lassitude, revealing a condition of weariness that was not recognized while the lash and command of duty urged us on. Here is one of the dangers of our climate. There are no days that freeze out the worker, none that burn him out. All days are favorable to business, and the year runs away with no excuse for any sound man not to be at his office, counter, or shop. The average active Californian of fifty years has probably done as much hard, unintermitted work as an Eastern man of the same class would have done at the age of sixty. We have more bald headed men to the thousand than any other community, probably. What is to be the effect of all this on posterity, is a question in heredity. Like trees like men, in the effect of climatic influence upon stamina. We produce no very hard woods. The ailanthus, eucalyptus, soft maple and soft oak are our product. The hickory, the gnarled white oak, do not abound. Close observers find that we are not raising a generation of hickory men and women. The cold and heat of Eastern States, the rougher conditions of life, are developing there a hardier race of men and women. We have as yet many of those who have been compacted amid the conditions named and a new influx is constantly pouring into our population. For this reason we do not see so clearly the effect of our climate upon vigor and endurance. But in these unquestionable facts we find a further hint of the need of frequent rest and change. At least twice a year a hard working business man should sleep and eat and breathe in another climate for as many days or as few as he can snatch from a busy life, a whole week at least.

Are you good at conundrums? Well, here is an original production. Why is this bush covered desert like the municipal council of—well, say New York, for instance, as well as for safety? Give it up? Well, so do I. Perhaps there is no resemblance. But as I have raised your expectations, I will say that the idea came into my head as I observed what a retreat it is for bitter sage hens. Bad as that is for a conundrum, it is still better than a pun Joe got off just now. Joe is a San Francisco drummer in the section opposite, an agreeable young man and a good traveling companion. Wife named one of the two horned toads that she added to her stock of pets just below here after him when he told her that he was born with horns on, but his mother sandpapered them off. Both Joe and the toad seem well pleased with the arrangement. Looking out at the window just now, he (Joe, not the toad), saw large flocks of sheep feeding on the almost perpendicular faces of the hills, hanging on by their toes, when he exclaimed, " What a country for hung mutton!"

What connection subsists between piety and clothes? The query arises as I look out of my window and study an ecclesiastic, a bishop from Japan on his way out to England to attend some convention, possibly the great Lambeth Convocation. He wears a soft, black felt hat, a flowing undercoat wrapped about him, and secured at the waist by a cord twice encircling and ending in large tassels, cut high with standing collar, an outside coat of same cut secured at the neck by a single button, and flowing freely on the breeze, trowsers ending in the tightest of leggings with buttons down the outside and secured by a leather strap under the instep. The whole rig, except his standing collar, is of the most somber and lusterless black. Again we ask, what connection is there between the tailor's shears and the conversion of the heathen? What degree of impressiveness in preaching the laws of God belong to one suit of clothes rather than to another? How much supplementary aid can the draper and tailor furnish to the theological seminary? Is there any sense in any man's making an unmitigated guy of himself ostensibly for the sake of Christ? Jesus did not so, nor did any of his apostles. Why should we? Certain proprieties all expect, and sensible men bow to them, but ultraisms excite ridicule and deserve all they get. Quite the opposite is the case of those who think that the Master is dishonored by any use of ornament or of dress beyond the very plainest. A flower on a lady's hat or a ring in her ear or on her finger is evidence to such minds of an unmortified state of heart, quite deplorable in a Christian. I have as little sympathy with this notion as with the other. Jesus probably dressed like any other carpenter's son, ornamentation included. We do not read that he instituted any dress reform. John the Baptist was out of the prevailing fashion, and a note is made of the fact. The whole truth, probably is, that where there is the adorning of a meek and quiet spirit the person is well dressed in the sight of God. After this their sanctified common sense must rule.

Some of the meekest spirits in the world have dressed beautifully, having ample means to do so, and desiring to please their friends. It makes no beautiful woman more pious to dress her like a fright, nor is she necessarily yielding to temptation, to vanity, when she improves her talent of beauty for the brightening up of this workaday world. I often wonder whether this proclamation of alliance between religion and poverty, between religion and voluntary plainness and homeliness, remanding to the devil so much that is beautiful and helpful and cheerful, so many of the good things of life for the sake of some spook of fear, is not an asceticism that is contrary to the spirit of Christ, and chargeable with creating a perverted notion of his true church on earth. Pure and true religion is one of the most sensible things in the world. It is loving and serving God with a sincere desire to please him. Did God wish this earth to be somber, then why did he create beautiful colors and beautiful flowers? Did he want men to exclude the voice of joy and gladness, then why the merry song of bird; why the joyfulness of everything purest and most like himself? No, no, friends, let us have done with all this. Make the earth beautiful, make it gladsome. Conscience will work as well when addressed by the power of a beautiful piety as when by one bowed down like a bulrush, and weeping like the ancient prophet. But I may not think as all do about this any more than about other matters, but I do think and speak as I think.

Crossing this continent is like visiting Niagara. It grows on one at each visit. More stupendous seems the undertaking that has made California what she is, and will yet make her one of the foremost States in the Union. I am very well content that they who overcame the obstacles and conquered mountain and desert for future thousands shall be greatly enriched. The smallest conceivable fraction of the wealth that they have made possible to the masses would make them richer still. Yet when one looks at the vastness of the work it is plainly evident that not man nor company built it, but the masses, the government, between whom and the constructors there should be a fair settlement of accounts. But do not think that I am riding on a free pass and am showing gratitude by these writings. Passes are issued to clergymen as well as to others, and to their wives, to my certain knowledge. But to the great mass the Interstate Commerce law is a convenient and effectual barrier. Yet how it vanishes when politics are to the front! Then a hint to the conductor written in pencil on a slip of brown paper, as I noted recently, is sufficient. Nor do I complain. A pass is an equivalent for services rendered or bid for. It always raises a question. The only fair thing to do is to treat all alike, and if favors are to be shown to any let it be to those on the Pacific coast who are building up the trade of the roads. Generally, however, they are sported by parties outside of this range, indicating the corrupt side of railroad influence in government circles.

But I have rambled on far enough for this time. Amid sunshine, hail, and snow we are now dashing, soon to revisit old scenes and old friends, amid whom and which I shall not forget my transcontinental loved ones and home.   FRANCIS A. HORTON.

LETTER II.

DENVER, MAY 7th, 1888.

For once in my life I am able to look down upon all my good friends in Oakland. It is not my nature to be high minded, but on the contrary, to borrow the language of a character who afforded me a fund of amusement in earlier days, "I am a very humbly man." But sometimes we cannot help getting up in the world. So here we are in Denver, Col., more than a mile higher up in the air than the top of the higher steeple of my church. And it is charming up here. The air is soft and smooth and pure, the lungs taking in great quantities of it with pleasure. At once a sound lunged person realizes what hope of continuance is here for the person of weak lungs. Yet there are limits. If the lung tissue is unimpaired all is well. But if disease has taken hold upon it this climate aggravates the case. But in many instances persons who have suffered from hemorrhage merely, have never had a return of the trouble after coming here to live. Yonder are the high peaks of the Rockies, eternally snow capped, acting as a refrigerator, sending to-day to us a cool breath full of vigor. Overhead the sun shines through long beautiful hours—in one word, it is as delightful a day as one ever finds anywhere. Of course, it takes more than one day to make a season, but judging from the sample we enjoyed I do not wonder at the remark of Mr. Tabor to me, (Mr. Tabor who built the Grand Opera House, and who has in other ways invested vast sums of money in the city:) "We have as fine a climate for twelve months in the year as can be found on earth."

Next to climate, in the make up of a city, comes the water supply, which in this case is abundant and of the purest quality. Artesian wells reach water at sixteen feet below the surface. As the boring proceeds new veins are struck, yielding at times mineral waters of high value, as, for instance, at the Winsor House, where a stream of water flows ceaselessly from a nine hundred foot well, which waters are said to be very beneficial in all cases of kidney troubles. The main dependence, of course, is upon the city water-works, which secure their supply in other ways. The water rates do not differ materially from those of the Contra Costa Company. Charges, however, are made out on a different plan, a certain monthly rental being assessed for household purposes, reaching throughout the twelve months, and an additional charge being made per month for irrigation purposes extending throughout the season of irrigation. Drainage, which is the next consideration, is here arranged for by nature, so that the system is well nigh perfect. The fall toward the streams in every direction is very considerable. In the item of building material, nature certainly has set her affection upon Denver. First, are the hills of brick clay which yield large supplies of good quality. Just now the prices are very stiff, good quality burnt brick selling at $9 per thousand, pressed brick being far more costly. A new residence was shown me, the pressed brick in which cost $32 per thousand. Then the marble yards are well stocked with good quality. Then the beautiful white and red sandstone is very abundant. But best of all to my mind is the lava stone. It has several peculiarities. It is a light weight stone, weighing some twenty pounds less to the cubic foot than the sandstone. It is also soft and easily wrought into shape for use. It has the quality, however, of hardening with age, so that each year the structure composed of it grows more secure. Then it has those beautiful tints coming from injection of mineral substances while in molten state. Some parts are as gray as the white sandstone, some as pink as the red sandstone, with many intermediate tints. With these facilities at hand a solid city is the outcome. Curbstones are stones in fact, sidewalks are made of sawn slabs of smooth stone, houses are of solid material. Combinations most pleasing are effected. Thus we see brick houses trimmed with pressed brick, white sandstone trimmed with red sandstone, and vice versa, lava in combination with red sandstone, and, perhaps, finished about the entrances with polished granite. The charming effect of all this multiplied on every side can be easily imagined.

In the building up of Denver it is further to be considered that the State of Colorado is in the mere infancy of its development. Its mineral resources are very great. Coal in abundance is found, but as yet of a poor quality, none having been found that will coke. Silver, gold, copper, iron, Spiegel iron in limited quantity, are here. Dr. Maynard of Cheyenne told me that he, with seven others, had laid claim under the Placer law of the State to a vein of kaolin several miles in length and some fourteen feet in breadth and depth, which was pure decomposed feldspar, absolutely destitue of iron or any other mineral that would tint the pure white porcelain that could be manufactured from it. I remarked to him that I remembered being told at Sevres, in France, some years ago, at the celebrated porcelain works, that atmosphere had much to do with their industry. The idea seemed new to him, and at his request I shall make more particular inquiry on this point during the next few months. The vast herding interests of Colorado are gradually taking on better shape. The tendency now is toward smaller herds and more care, with less hardship and loss in winter. Blessed be pockets which men will regard even when the lowing of starving and freezing dumb creatures fall on hardened ears. I saw at the foot of one telegraph pole by the wayside the dead bodies of five full grown cattle lying where they fell. As all the interests of the State proceed in their rapid developement, Denver will feel the impulse and rise with the flood tide. This is all the more certain because eastward there is no city of importance until Kansas City is reached, and westward nothing to compete with it until we reach Salt Lake City. Thus with natural advantages, with un-limited resources, and with geographical position everything is in favor of a great, strong, and beautiful city. It all depends upon the people, and what they intend to do is well indicated by what they have done and are doing. The business atmosphere is full of ozone. The city is less than 30 years old, but has made for itself already a name. Note the one fact concerning the vast union depot, which is now too small and is about to be enlarged, as indicating how the business men take their own city in hand and govern matters amicably, as though they had something to say about things. This fact is that the depot and grounds belong to the city, and not to the railroads, the right to lay and use tracks being given by the city to the roads. Of course it is to the interest of the city to give the roads all the facilities they need for the transaction of business. It is a mutual affair, but the position of the city is one of much honor and safety therein. Heavy smelting works roll their dense smoke upwards, and the roar and whiz of manufacture are heard. Business blocks of vast size and beauty and costliness are going up to add to the numbers of such already built and occupied. When a city without a boom can afford to pull down good two and three story structures to erect far better ones, there is some foundation of prosperity under it. This is nature's boom. The

Tabor Opera House surpasses in beauty and extravagance of finish any similar structure in San Francisco. And it is used. The seven performances of the Booth-Barrett combination yielded $29,000. The new Denver Club building is the gem of the city. The dry goods house of Daniels & Fisher, externally and internally, would be a conspicuous object if placed on Market street. It is more like my memory of Lord & Taylor's of New York than anything seen since. The hotels are roomy and well appointed.

In the matter of churches the city is wonderfully developed. St. John's Cathedral is specially noticeable, cruciform, with beautiful windows, soft fresco, splendid organ. Trinity Methodist, far larger, not yet completed, the organ of which is intended to be the largest in America, the gift of one man, a former Californian, Mr. Blake. The Presbyterian churches likewise are fine structures, and, better than all, the spacious buildings are filled on each Sabbath at both services.

The school buildings are very fine, especially the two High school buildings, which are large enough to serve as capitols for a young State. The county buildings also are on the same scale. I walked over the foundations of the new State Capitol, from which it is easy to see what is the thought of the architect. Private residences run up high into the thousands of dollars of cost in many cases. Over two thousand houses were built last year, and the city is extending. The Baptists have located their college out Colfax avenue as far as Mountclair, and the Wolff private school has secured a location near the same point. A cable line out Colfax is in the near future, and prosperity is moving along that entire line. New cities are the marvel of America's progress, and among them none excites more wonder and admiration than Denver. F. A. HORTON.

LETTER III.

ALBANY, MAY, 11th. 1888.

From the roof of the great hardware house of Horton, Gilmore, McWilliams & Co., Lake street, as far as the eye can see before us lies new Chicago. Without doubt the fire that swept over this vast area was one of the fiercest on record. When wood goes up in smoke and ashes like shavings, there is some fire raging. When iron runs down like water there is intense heat in the conflagration. When brick melts we approach the limits of our ability to measure heat. But when a tongue of flame, fed by choicest combustibles and driven by a blast, touches stone and it snaps and crackles like powder under the match and then melts and runs down like molten glass, we have the climax of combustion in the open air. I well remember passing through here a few days after the worst was over, while yet great mountains of anthracite coal were blazing, and smoke and steam were ascending from numberless pits that once were cellars; when ashes and soot and blackness were on every side; when bridges were down, and over wide acres upon acres there was no sign of the city that had gone up. I look over it to-day, and, more marvelous than Arabian Nights, here stands without doubt, in solid blocks, the best built city in the world. Every man vied with his neighbor to build larger, costlier, and better than he. Nothing small and mean and cheap detracts from the magnificent. New York is richer and greater in many ways; Boston has more culture, probably. Philadelphia may have the best blood, but in vigor and enterprise and business courage and undertaking Chicago leads them all.

As an instance the conduct of the head of this firm under our feet has always been quoted by those who were conversant with the facts. He was at the time of the fire low down in the firm of William Blair & Co., an old and established house doing an enormous business on the most conservative principles. Awakened at the dead of night by word that fire was rapidly approaching the store he hastily arose and went down town, but the sea of fire encircled their house so that he could come nowhere near to it. For a moment he viewed its destruction from a distance, then grasping the situation he turned his back upon the scene that was wiping out their past and set to work to shape a future. He remembered seeing recently a very large brick building outside the fire circle just approaching completion. Hunting up the owner he leased it at less than $10,000 per annum. Then striking off a business circular, he drummed up a printer and set him at work throwing them from his press. Then far and wide over the country he telegraphed his orders for new stock, and when morning broke his house was on its feet again. The old store was still a mass of red ruins, unapproachable for many squares, when the new was already a success. With the opening of business hours came the carpenters to put up the shelving and other necessary appurtenances. Then came telegrams from all quarters announcing goods on the way, and generally ending with " Hurrah for Chicago!" " Bully for you!" " Go in and win!" and other such sentiment. Also now came throngs of business men seeking quarters and offering almost any price for accommodation. Thirty thousand dollars rent could easily have been taken for the block, but the answer always came, " We pay so much for the building; William Blair & Co. cannot afford to make money out of such distress as now prevails ; whatever space we do not require is at your disposal, and we will apportion the rent agreed upon according to accommodation." Such grit and good spirit rebuilt the city, and this is the living spirit in its wheels of progress. By and by this grand store was enriched with an increasing trade. Then with the revolving years Mr. Nelson fell asleep, and Mr. Blair, full of years and wealth, retired, and Mr. Horton came to the head. Associating with himself younger men, backed by vast capital, he pushed on to greater development the house he has shown himself so well qualified to command. A poor boy from a country village, he has won every step of his progress by the excellence of his character and by dint of the hardest knocks. Such men should be a living inspiration to youth of both sexes. Be honest, be capable, be gritty, and success will make you her best bow.

Nevertheless, when beauty is up for remark, big, busy, bustling Chicago must give place to Cleveland, the elegant. Soft with warm spring showers, wooed by strong sunbeams, her continuous lawns, close shaven, are at their greenest, the maples and elms are springing to leaf. Choice crocuses and pansies and violets, vanguard of the great floral army that is marching northward, have already pitched their welcome tents. Here is the home of Dr. C. S. Sprecher, my esteemed predecessor in the First Presbyterian Church of Oakland. The same success that attended him there and in San Francisco still waits upon him here. His evening audiences are steadily increasing. Here also is my monument in the Case Avenue Presbyterian Church, the result of nine years of hard labor, a monument that will abide even should fire destroy the building of Amherst stone. No work is so lasting as that which is done for

God and humanity. No friendships can compare with those formed amid such associations. And within this circle the very strongest are found where the members are few and the work is great, where labors and denials are daily experiences and hope delayed makes the heart sick. Then the chaff is blown away by the rough gales of circumstance and the winnowed grain alone abides. Heart joins to heart, hand to hand, and through all sunderings of subsequent days the link of golden friendship firmly holds.

What more natural, then, than that I should at once upon arrival drop in on Captain Kendall of the regular army, now retired? What more in harmony with good form than that, after their first breath of surprise, they should say: "Must you go right on to-morrow? Well, then, we will summon the old guard to dinner here to-night." And such of them as could be reached came and a happy time we had. Harness imagination to thought and draw no rein over the foam flecked steeds until within the better country ahead. Do you see yon animated group interested most of all in themselves? They are an "old guard," whose friendships, surviving the wreck of fortune, the flight of time, the waste of disease, the crumbling to dust of the temple of the body, are strongest now and reformed for all eternity.

The growth of the anti-saloon sentiment in Ohio is wonderful. And the most interesting feature of it all is that the Republican party is making it an issue before the people. The wind is being taken from the sails of the Prohibitionists, men who have become restive to an almost insufferable degree under the inactivity of the Republican party on this question are now being reassured and are returning to their allegiance with joy. The fear of losing the German vote has passed away, and, indeed, of losing anything. The sentiment of the State is rising, so that there is more to gain than to lose by an open advocacy of local option. Many small centers, where liquor has dominated from time unreckoned, have been c'eaned out at the ballot box, and now in a quiet way, but with great momentum, the drift of thought is toward a vote by wards in the great cities. Out of ten wards in almost any city seven would vote no liquor. This would throw the selling and drinking into the other three. This would so depreciate property by the comparison, by the moving out of better classes, that sooner or later, in self defense, those wards would join the others.   If not, then crimes would be concentrated there, police patrol would be multiplied there, criminal statistics would point almost to the very doors where crime is fostered.   Why cannot our good friends of the Prohibition party join us in working up to some such point?   Ohio has not done this in a day.   Why insist upon conquering the rebellion in the battle of some one day?   Ohio has a Sunday law and is using it with effect in this campaign.   California should have one too.   Free-thinkers hoot at the idea because it has a savor of religion about it.   They might as well hoot at conscience for the same reason.   The Adventists oppose it with all their vigor, and stand arrayed against the party of national reform and against the progress of the anti-saloon movement.   The more is the pity.   Others for other reasons are in the same class, but two things are clear in the future sky of California, viz : There will be a Sabbath law and the saloons must retire.   The rising sentiment will before long overflow its banks and sweep in a deluge of life over our wide plains.   May God speed the day.

Phew !   How we are flying through New York State on the limited !   If I find anything finer than this in my travels in the way of railroading, I shall make a note of it.   But don't set your heart on the note.   I think it will not come.   Palace day coaches, vestibuled, with dining car, stopping on an average once in eighty-eight miles, and going like Tam O'Shanter running away from the witches, over a smooth road well ballasted, having four tracks, insuring safety against collision, all this is a combination not easily found.   More than all, I have in my pocket a pair of those little conveniences which the unaccustomed Britisher calls "brasses," but which we invented and call checks.   FRANCIS A. HORTON.

LETTER IV.

PHILMONT, N. Y., May 15th.

Dear Robin Redbreast, why does he not come to Oakland to live ? the children would love him, he would be so happy skipping over our lawns with his 'Dot-and-go-one" hop, worms and fruit are there in satisfying abundance, why does he not come?   Yonder in the old pine trees just above this house where I was born, is singing now one of those beautiful creatures his evening hymn. Oh! how it chirps and swells and trills and rolls. I fancy that he is singing a welcome home to me; he certainly found his keynote in my heart. Doubtless he is a lineal descendant of those who have summered in that tree for generations. So tame were they that they would get in the way of the hoe in their eagerness to secure the fat earthworm. Dear fellow, how you carry me back along the track of time. How you cover again the fields that border the laughing Occawamuc with dense and primeval forests, broken only here and there by settlements. I see the young and handsome bride with her stalwart husband coming here to find a home. Your ancestors sang bridal carols for them morning and night. I see the first baby in its cradle, an occasion of wonder and curiosity to the dark, savage men, silent but friendly, who enter unannounced at any hour. I see them lift it in their strong arms while the mother stands by a picture of smiling agony, smiling in order not to show fears or distrust, agony at the spectre of a possibility that they might walk off with it. While you sing the panoramic years roll on. The scene changes; the forests are no more, save in the rocky fastnesses about the great falls where madly leaps the Occawamuc to a lower level a sheer hundred feet. Wild scenery, full of inspiration! One cannot help singing, cannot help imagining great deeds. Its roar is like the tread of hosts, its shock and tremble are like the colliding of mighty forces, the soughing of the wind evermore through the trees is the music of the eternal battle. The red man now has gone, the wild stream is tamed, and you, robin, who sang its days of freedom, sing now its days of fettered industry, as, like a blind old Sampson at his mill, it turns the multiplied wheels of manufacture.

Then came my day. As along these waters I rambled with rod and line you sang for me. As through these meadows I hunted the luscious strawberry, small but sweet, you with Robert of Lincoln kept me company. In later years, when in this deep cave I made my first study and set me down to write my earliest sermon, you were my choirmaster. The murmuring waters rippling past its mouth filled up the melody, and ever since in all my later efforts I think I can detect the echo of your early encouragement, and the deep, soothing murmur of the heart of nature, that covers all defects and tones all into harmony. The panorama rolls and still you sing, and now that bride of yore, our aged and beloved mother, dies, and with our tears your plaintive expressions of grief were mingled, and your song has ever since contained to me a tear. And when yesterday we turned aside into the churchyard to stand awhile by mother's grave, that tenderest spot on earth to manly heart, that place where earth'and heaven closest join, dear, dear old Rob, there we found you, your lone watch keeping. And well you may, for well she loved you. Keep thus near the gate of heaven, Rob; it will be pleasanter to have you therein, and I think that you shall be there. Does not tradition truly say that you found your red breast by sympathetic contact with the bleeding side of the Man of Sorrows as he bled to open heaven? Heaven's own bird, paradise is not too good for you. A seraph might do worse than pluck enough of down from his soft wing to make old Rob a nest.

"Change and decay on all around I see" as I move about among the scenes of my childhood. The old oaken bucket has gone, the very well has gone, the garden that lay near it has gone, all given up to other uses. The grand old hills that gave such sport to us coasters when winter covered them with snow and glaring ice are made now to bow their heads and consent to easier grades. The stream that went dancing and glinting along is a reservoir now, a change as from frolicsome boy to sober man. The farms are village sites now, and cottages supplant the waving grain. The farmers, too, are gone, save where now and then one sees an aged man leaning on his staff or draws nearer to hear him talk of the good old quiet times of the long ago. In what I see and tell I touch the heart of many an Oaklander whose experience coincides with mine or whose fear of such experience delays his footsteps of return to the old home. Each present place and present station are all that we may call our own. No deed to property can hold it to us the very same through years. Men may not rob us of it, but time and change will eat away its very self so that while the semblance remains the thing itself has escaped, even as the pile stands firm and sound to the eye while the teredo has really carried it away. Nature buries our past and begins to dig its grave as soon as we are advanced one single step, grazes our heel as she strikes in her hasty spade, old grave digger that she is. Would that she could bury many of our doings that memory recalls as easily as she buries our belongings.

But as though by contrast with our evanishing to set forth her own perduring, we have but to lift our eye and there stretches away the lofty range of the Catskills. From childhood we have studied them and to-day there is no elevation, no depression that is not an old familiar object. Deep lie the shadows on the Kaaterskill clove, while sweeping nobly upwards and northward rounds the high top of North mountain, on whose northern slope stands out the Catskill Mountain House, now entering upon its sixty-sixth year. On its southern slope stands the new Kaaterskill in full view. Rome has its legends and we laugh at them, but to this day great foundations stand in close connection with events as puerile as a suckling mother wolf. Thus the celebrated house last named sprang from a chicken (a spring chicken, but we forbear to pun).

One day at the Mountain House a guest ordered spring chicken and was informed that he could not have it. He made a rumpus and was told that if he wanted spring chicken he had better build an hotel of his own and furnish it. He vowed that he would, and he did, and the Kaaterskill is the magnificent result of that quarrel. It is said that their bill of fare is never without spring chicken. Such antics hot blooded men can play, even among the clouds on nature's always solemn and impressive high places. But to stand on that piazza of the old Mountain House and look off. Oh ! what a vision ! The Hudson winding along for full seventy miles, the Berkshire hills to the east shutting in the scene, the Fishkill range to the south, the Adirondacks to the north, and the Catskill under our feet and rolling up high behind us, the wide valley laid as on the flat surface of a map with wood and cultivated field and stream and lovely home as far as the eye can see. And now the deep thunder breaks, but it is below us, the sun is glorious overhead, but from north and south up and down the valley move the cloud armies, and now they approach nearer ; now the forked lightning flashes across, the fierce artillery of the skies ; the peal follows, louder, quicker ; we hear the rain falling on the tree tops below, but still over us the sun shines on, another instance of the upper ten thousand in sunshine, the lower five in misery. They mingle, they are too close for cannonading any longer, they blend and become a sea, and fill the valley to our very feet with a luminous waste of apparent waters, with surface broken into billows by the passing gale. Yet from beneath those cloud waves come strange sounds of life, lowing of herds, shouts of workmen, and the like, with strange weird effect as though we were gazing into some hades, impenetrable to vision yet which the ear peoples with life. There to the south lies the Old Man of the Mountain, flat on his back, his forehead, eyebrows, sockets, nose, lips, chin, neck, all clean cut. His swelling breast is a mighty ridge, his raised knee is a lofty peak, his foot a noble spur of the range. From change and decay to such surroundings we cheerfully turn, glad to be reminded that there are some things that do not change. Thus, prophet and poet have ever arisen from their tasks for and among men to reassure their souls by something steadfast. Then have they turned to the mountains, and from them by an easy transition to him who laid their deep foundations. To the lover of nature the mountains are an un-wearying attraction.

To the farming population these mountains serve as a barometer. When one arises in the morning the first thing to do is to look at them. By their nearness or remoteness the state of the atmosphere is judged and the character of the day prognosticated. If clouds hang on them the position of the clouds is significant, and a note is made whether they form a "nightcap" for the peaks or a " belt" for the middle. If the clouds are moving, the direction they take shows whether rain or dry may be expected. Thus for long years they are man's companion, and one cannot wonder at the sense of homesickness experienced by such when removed from them. As one expressed it who returned from the more level west, "I couldn't stand it; it seemed as though the gable end was kicked out of all creation." When to love for them one adds that of the noble Hudson, the imperial Hudson, that flows along their base, an idea can be formed of the strength of the spell that binds all residents to their homes in these localities. Moving amid these old familiar scenes, I feel the awaking love, and strike a compromise with my heart by saying, every place has its compensating advantages ; nature has left none entirely out in the cold.

FRANCIS A. HORTON.

LETTER V.

PHILADELPHIA, May 25.

At last we are in our Presbyterian Jerusalem. This is hallowed soil to our church. Here was created our republic, with which our Presbyterian fathers had much to do, as was only natural, for Presbyterianism is essentially republicanism, as Anglicanism is essentially monarchical and Romanism is essentially despotic, in tendency. Here was formed the first presbytery in the United States, here was formed the first synod, and here was formed the first assembly, which convened in 1788, just one hundred years ago. Here also, in the year 1870, was celebrated the grand reunion of the old and new schools, which took place in the very church wherein the opening exercises of this Centennial Assembly occured on the 17th inst. There are to-day within the limits of this city Presbyterian churches of all kinds to the number of 104. Every fifth person met npon the streets, man, woman and child, is a Presbyterian, and none of them look very blue, either. This is the place where Presbyterians never do look blue. Our denomination alone has here 106 Sabbath schools, containing 42,562 members. The churches are substantial, the newer ones quite beautiful. But no attempt is made to keep pace with the wondrous beauty and costliness of many of the public and corporation buildings. In this respect Philadelphia stands quite alone. Solidity, massiveness, costliness, and beauty combine in many public buildings to a rare degree.

The churches are well attended at the morning service, and in some instances where less exhaustion of energy is occasioned by religious work on the part of the people, or where more energy is put into the service on the part of the pastor, both services are full. Among all of our local men here, I am informed by a competent critic, John Hemphill, formerly of San Francisco, is the most popular and best "all round" preacher, and has the largest audiences. This will be a good word to his many friends on the Pacific coast where he lived for thirteen years.

The assembly is in full blast. From Puget sound to Mexico, from Boston to North Carolina, and from all regions between commissioners are in attendance. From far off lands they have come. The Supreme Court of the United States, the Gubernational Chair of Pennsylvania, the Territorial Commission of Washington Territory, the National Senate, the judicial bench of Minnesota contribute to its membership. Editors, professors, lawyers, doctors, preachers, bankers, men from all the branches of industry which Presbyterians engage are here to the number of nearly 600. Hospitality has been extended to 1500 in immediate connection with the assembly. It is a very strong body. Some of the old men are here, some of the younger men are here, but the mass is composed of the burden bearers, the destiny shapers of the church. Men long separated meet again and refresh their memories of the days of old lang syne. The lobbies present animated scenes. Very many ladies are in attendance in the interests of missions or simply in company with their husbands to share in the celebrations.

The auspicious day opened without a cloud. The air was pleasant and cool, the sun filtered through the opening leaves of the trees and fell in golden patches upon the walks. The body met at Horticultural Hall and, augmented to a force of 1500 by visitors, quietly marched by twos up Brook street to Washington square to the First church. It was a typical Presbyterian procession. There was no brass band with brazen clamors of pride and ostentation ; there were no flaunting banners thrown to the breeze; there was nothing to indicate who or what the body of men were, nor why they were here, nor why the city was so moved at their presence. They needed nothing of the sort in these surroundings. Their name, their character, their history, were household words. Before that vast assemblage Ex-moderator Dr. Smith arose and in fitting words announced his text as that upon which Dr. Witherspoon had preached at the first assembly one hundred years ago, viz: 1 Cor. iii, "Neither is he that planteth anything nor he that watereth, but God that giveth the increase." Of course plowing, watering, and increasing were lines along which the noble discourse ran the history of the past century in our church life and progress. Grand old man, his sermon was one that any younger man might envy, his mellifluous delivery rings in pleasing cadences in my ear still. I could not help saying, "What need is there to speak of a dead line at fifty or sixty years for the preacher when men of such advanced age have still such power." There is no dead-line except when a man ceases to think and study. This may come at thirty, or may never come, as the man himself shall select.

Kansas City gives to us the Moderator in the person of Dr. Thompson. He was chosen in part because he represents the "Far West." It is very amusing, and now and then not a little provoking, to see how little the average man east of the Rocky mountains knows of the far West. The patronizing manner, not to say the half pitying manner, in which we are referred to it is sometimes hard to endure. And it does no good to explain, for their minds are made up about it, and any description of affairs with another coloring is discredited. I took occasion to speak up for California in the matter of education after some good New York man had appealed to the body to come to our rescue in the matter of education lest we should grow up in illiteracy, and at table in the hotel a couple of hours later I had the pleasure of having one of my best friends, who sat with his back to me and was unaware of my presence, say, "Horton must have made that a little rose colored." This was offset by a confession by Dr. Worden, who heard me speak of California affairs at Minneapolis two years ago. He had the same opinion of my statements, but since that day he has visited California, with his estimable wife, and now makes a voluntary confession to me that I did not tell one half of the case. So little by little, Eastern eyes are opening.

The interest in the question of fraternal relations with the Presbyterian Church South was the culminating point. It was looked ahead to for weeks; ever since the publication of the official correspondence between the committees of the two assemblies, which for urbanity, loftiness, and diplomacy is not often equaled. Then the committees of arrangements provided for an all day meeting of the two bodies in two places in this City, to be presided over and addressed by Northern and Southern men, turn and turn about, on great vital questions of church life and progress. Before this day came an invitation was extended to both assemblies from Mr. and Mrs. Wistar Morris of Overbrook to meet at their residence and be received. This was accepted. Upon this came another invitation to attend a joint reception at the Academy of Fine Arts. The first was set for Wednesday afternoon, the 23d inst., the second for the evening of the same day, the following day being the great day of joint celebration before mentioned. These arrangements were carried out to the very letter. We met and fraternized and learned to respect each other. The Northern Church wore blue silk badges, small, chaste, and suitably inscribed with gilt letters with name of our body. The Southern brethren wore white badges with a transverse diagonal bar of blue. Wherever in the vast throng of more than 5000 people the badged men met there was no waiting for a farther introduction, but palm met palm and brotherhood was established on the spot. Amid the highest works of art in the many rooms we moved about, with flowers on every side, the band discoursing sweet music, and the spirit of true brotherhood over all. Every one voted it a great success. After a good night's rest, the morning broke on the day of days.

The rain came down copiously, but no one heeded it. The feast was spread and every one chose his place. We studied the programme and chose Horticultural Hall. Here a son of old Dr. Robert J. Breckinbridge, a member of Congress from Kentucky, led off in an address upon "Calvinism and Liberty." The spirit of his father seemed to rest upon him. Large, graceful, with snow white hair and full beard, he held that immense throng spell-bound under one of the finest specimens of sustained oratory to which I have ever listened. Bursts and rolls of applause cheered him on from period to period, and when he had finished it rose to an ovation. He came forward and gracefully acknowledged the compliment on behalf of the truth he had uttered. Let no man ever say, while such men and such themes meet, that oratory is a lost art. Impassioned utterances of lofty and far reaching truth thrill and electrify to-day as at any period of the world's history. Then came on Howard Crosby of New York, who was introduced as being "every inch a scholar and every inch a man," who, amid great demonstrations of admiration, opened the subject of " Presbyterianism and Biblical Scholarship." He went headlong after the men who bow down to the continent and regard "German indorsement as a title to intellectual nobility." Near him sat some of those who are given to evolving wonderful things from their own "inner consciousness," who are victims of "intellectual inebriety," who discuss the scriptures "as having been on the ground when they were given," into whose notions he poured hot shot for the space of forty minutes. It was a rare treat, and between him and Mr. Breckinridge the honors were easy and the audience in raptures

In the afternoon Dr. John Hall opened up the subject of " City Evangelization" in his clear and forcible manner. He was followed by Dr. Hoge of Richmond, Va., upon a kindred theme. Tall, lank, angular, with high cheekbones, a pinched face, and sharp nasal tones, he has yet the true oratorical fire burning within him, and held the close attention of the house for three quarters of an hour. A very pretty little passage occurred between him and Dr. Hall, showing how keenly alive is the body to anything that smacks of union. Dr. Hall explained how he had tried to induce Mr. Jessup to take his place, and how he resisted his pastor. "So," said he, " when two great bodies come together it is necessary that each give way a little." The assembly caught it, and made the welkin ring. "Be not so hasty in your generalization," said Dr. Hall, "I was only speaking of personal matters." And then the applause was louder. When Dr. Hoge came to speak he referred to the two churches, remarking: "They are not one, nor yet are two, but both look alike as sisters do." Then he added, "they not for that reason marry each other, they may prefer to marry some one else." The crowd caught the idea again and when the noise had subsided somewhat he sharply added, "Be not too hasty in your generalization. I was merely speaking of personal matters."

Time would fail to speak the great and gifted men who took part in the discussion. Dr. Cuyler's paper on foreign missions was lauded to the skies. The church in Christ for a lost world out of Christ was one of his epigrams that will resound down along Presbyterian halls for many days to come. The next day the debate on organic union ran high, the final conclusion being to enlarge the committee, accept its report, adopt substantially its provisions, and pass them along another year. The result was entirely unanimous and was announced amid long continued applause. No one doubts that the events of the past few days have mightily strengthened the bonds of love between the churches north and south. God's own good day is coming on, we would not hasten it unduly, then when it comes it will bring in the desire of all hearts without a root of bitterness anywhere.

The immense Academy of Music is packed every time it is opened for a popular meeting in connection with any of the great benevolent works of our church. Home missions and Foreign missions take the palm and the very best speakers attainable address the throngs. Take it for all in all we do not expect to see so glorious

an assembly again.   Its inspiration will lift the entire church in its
work for many years to come.

Now we are up and away.   The good ship Alaska sails on Tues-
day for Queenstown, and by the time this reaches you some one
may be addressing old ocean in the language of an admiring
sufferer:

> O, deep, deep, mighty deep,
> I give thee what I cannot keep.
> Alas, let us hope for better things.

FRANCIS A. HORTON.

LETTER VI.

PROMENADE DECK, UNION LINE S. S. ALASKA, }
                                        June 4, 1888. }

Once upon a time Dr. Talmage crossed the Atlantic when the
sea was so smooth and charming that he wrote an article in its praise
entitled "The Smile of the Sea." I greatly fancy that the sea laughed
in its sleeve while he was doing it, for when he came home it treated
him so meanly that he says he has ever since been mad to think
that he wrote that letter.   Remembrance of that fact warns me to
be cautious.   The present temptation, however, is to laudatory ob-
servations; we shall only say, therefore, that if the sea is so minded it
can be most agreeable, and thus only have we found it on this voyage.
Never was a sail down the Hudson on the palatial steamer Drew or
on the St. John more quite than have been portions of this passage.
It is the poetry of motion, and barring the fog on the Banks and
the deafening whistle at two minutes intervals, there is not the least
thing to occasion inconvenience or to mar the pleasure.   Some people are in bed, of course.   The Alaska is a remarkably steady ship.
In the sea that now is on she does not list enough to deflect a quoit
in the game of shuffle board.   This is a point that ladies should note,
for ordinarily they fear the rolling motion more than the pitching.

In every other respect also she is a charming vessel.   Her appoint-
ments are complete, her saloon is large, her table well spread, her service cheerful and obliging, her decks are broad, with long ranges for
the necessary daily constitutional, her officers inspire confidence by
their close attention to duty, and last, but not least, she does not

loiter on her course. On the contrary she is a spinner, making about four hundred miles per day. This of course is not the swiftest time made by any steamer, but it is well up towards the head of the list and will satisfy all reasonable demands. We heartily commend her to all our friends who comtemplate the ocean passage.

What a world by itself a passenger's list contains. He who may wish to prosecute character studies will here find an ample field. There, for example, yonder is Senator Stanford of California with his wife. He is quite dignified, courteous, and kind. Nothing about his person or manner indicates that he is a distinguished member of the United States Senate. His name is not on the printed list of pas-sengers. There is no asumption of rights above any other person and no self seclusion. He sits on deek in a chair, like the rest of us, eats at the regular table, and orders from the same bill of fare, takes a walk with his wife in the jolly crowd like any other man of the people. Yet his face shows to a close student of physiognomy that he was not intended to do things in a small way, and the whole set of his features shows a determination as pronounced as his modesty.

Behind me at table is a hilarious group, composed of three Roman Catholic priests and several men with whom they seem to be boon companions. This morning I was taking an early walk on deck before breakfast with one of these gentlemen when Father Kelley approached and the following amusing conversation took place.

"The top o' the morning to ye, Father."

"The top o' the morning to yourself."

" And did ye hear burglars in the night?"

" No, and were there burglars?"

" Indeed there were, and you ought to be happy this morning in that ye saved two lives."

"Now ye surprise me ; and how did I save two lives?"

"Well, thin, this was the way of it. My room mate and myself was that thirsty in the night that we were about to die. Indeed it was a clear case that we should expire before the morning. We had never a drop and we knew that the bar was shut, so that our case was hopeless indeed. Then a thought struck me and I said to my room mate, if now, we can get around to Father Kelly's room, we can surely find the medicine that will keep us alive. So we went about to your room and found the door unfastened. We were the burglars, Father, and we searched not long until I had my hand on a neat demijohn, and I poured out a full glass, and took a small pony myself, and gave a good one to my friend, and the remainder to the Steward, who saw us, so that he would not report our doings to the Captain. And now early in the morning I haste to make full confession and ask your absolution."

"No sin has been committed," was the ready reply, "and no absolution is required, in this that ye did not awaken me, for I was having a swate sleep and had ye disturbed me it would have been an unpardonable sin, but inasmuch as ye did not awaken me, no sin was committed and no forgiveness need be asked."

Father Kelly strolled away smiling down the deck and I asked, "Is all this a morning joke?"

"No, indeed," was the reply, "it is all fact just as stated. My business calls me to test liquors and I can say that the brandy referred to was the finest which I have tasted for many a day."

Our captain is a splendid study. He has not been in the sight of the passengers since we started, his chair has not been turned in the saloon once thus far. We ran into fog soon after leaving Sandy Hook and have been in it ever since. He has two sharp-eyed men on the bow, two more on the promenade deck forward, two officers and a quartermaster on the bridge, one or two in the crow's nest, besides the man at the wheel. Eight or nine pairs of sharp eyes peer into the fog on every side to detect the approach of danger. And this is well, for under his care is a valuable ship with costly cargo, together with many scores of human lives. What an example of watchfulness. How easy to moralize. Darkness and fog are over human life ever league of our voyage, there can be no sense of security, no promise of safety, no hope of making our haven, unless we multiply our lookouts on the bow, on the deck, on the foremast, and on the bridge.

Many a young man is forging ahead with the breath of icebergs on his brow, with fog and darkness lying on his course, with no calm eye peering into his future. If he shall come safely to a desired port it will be a miracle. "Oh! I'll come out all right," is his watchword. Most surely do we hope so, but this is a great, deep, cruel sea of life over which we sail. Young man, you had better keep a lookout at your bow.

"You look bad this morning" said the big fat man with short

sack coat and ample trousers (why will fat men persist in wearing such short coats) to the young, well dressed man at his side. "You would look bad, too," said he, "if you had been as drunk as I was last night!" I saw him this morning in the smoking saloon playing poker with small stakes on the table. "Do you go abroad on business?" said a man to him. "No" was the proud reply, "I don't have to travel for business or follow any occupation." I could not help thinking of his father and mother, whether they had saved up money with this end in view—whether such an outcome of their life's labor would please them. A thousand times better would it have been had they turned all their money into gold and sailed out here into midocean, and in the name of their son, and for his sake, have thrown it as a cursed thing into the deep. There is a pitiable mistake here that is being repeated constantly. Every boy, as we say in California, should be required to rustle for himself, especially those who show a disposition to spend the "governor's" money. Hardworking parents naturally desire to make things a little easier for their children, to which end they dig and delve, they pinch and save, all through life. Of the outside world they know almost nothing. The culture and enlargement of ideas that travel brings they deny to themselves, because they think that they cannot afford it, while often at the end of life they see their mistake and say if I had to do it over I should act differently. A good education and sound moral and religious training are every child's due. When these are secured then there should be a generous participation by parents and children alike in the comforts and advantages that the family purse can buy. One such person of a working and saving turn, whose money has never given her the advantages it ought, while her sons have used and misused the most of it, said to me with mournfulness in tone, but none in word: "Frank, take the best, it is all in a lifetime." And I believe the path of wisdom for parents lies along a broad, generous provision for themselves, and for their family each day as it rolls away, with a prudent eye to oncoming age, and, perhaps, depleted income. The sweet joy of using money for good purposes in charity, or for the spread of the gospel, such people never taste. Sermons setting forth such needs are "begging" sermons, a term dishonorable alike to speaker and hearer. Money given by such is too often like throwing a joint at the head of a hungry dog that makes him yelp with pain before he can get his dinner. When having denied oneself the pleasures and advantages that money can secure, when having lost the opportunity it affords to do good, there is added the squandering habits of children tending to their destruction—the outcome of such a life of toil and saving is mournful in the extreme.

A very comfortable programme for a day's round of affairs on shipboard is a salt water bath at 7 A. M., hot, luke warm, or cold, as one elects, followed by a brisk walk or other active exercise until 8 o'clock. Then games, walking, reading, chatting, or snoozing on deck in reclining chairs, taking a cup of strong beef tea about 11:30 o'clock, with lunch at 1 P. M. Then after lunch nap in true navy style, followed by more careful toilet and exercise until dinner at 6 P. M. More exercise, etc., until night falls then to the dining saloon for music or books or writing and to bed at a right early hour. This is the best lay out, but in case stress of weather prevails then do the best you can regardless of order or ceremony. The best is monotonous, to wait is unspeakable.

From the dawn of literature the sea has been prolific of symbols. Its vastness strikes the mind of the beholder. Eternity is a sea, limitless, fathomless, engulfing. A Sabbath school teacher in Philadelphia told me that she took her class of poor children to see the ocean. One little girl stood and looked long, while her little breast heaved, until when interrupted by the question what she thought of it, she replied: "Well, mam, its the first time in my life that I ever had enough of anything." Its solitariness, so lonely, so desolate, so barren, so dreary, is painful to contemplate. Apart from the habitations of man it lies, hiding deep secrets forever in its own keeping, deep answering to deep in endless conversation with itself. The voyagings of men seem like intrusions into its solitudes, met by tossings and tumblings or, in angrier moods, by awful shipwreck. A grim, gloomy hermit is the sea, an ogre not pleasant to confront, nor safe to offend. Its distress awakens wonder. Why is it so troubled, why does it never rest, why does it moan so piteously, why does it beat so distressfully upon the sands, why in its deeper solitudes apart from habitations of men, does it shrink and wail and burst into frantic upheavals of passion? The heart of the wicked man, his conscience, "is like the troubled sea that cannot rest, but casts up mire and dirt." Its deceitfulness is proverbial. How it smiles and ripples and dances and lures. Come play in my breakers, come sail over my billows, so freely flowing, so smoothly rolling, but there is the undertow, that like a giant creature wraps its mighty arms about one's limbs and drags us down to death. There is the sudden squall, the outward flowing tide, the overturned boat, the floating corpses. Its remorselessness is dreadful. Pity does not dwell in its bosom. After all the ships it has swallowed down, all the misery it has caused it is as wicked and hardened as ever and as eager for havoc. Beautiful woman, tender child, alike fail to awaken sympathy. And yet its pureness is lauded, it has salt in itself, it ceaselessly tosses up its waters to the sun that his beams may penetrate and clarify them. And being pure the world is healthy. A putrid sea would give us a dead world right speedily. Its wisdom too is confessed. It visits every land under the sun, it speaks in every language used by human beings, tell tale rivers and brooks from every deep mountain fastness are pouring into its ear their gossip. Its informants come whence human foot has never trodden. And from the ages it has been gathering up its stores of knowledge. How it laughs as it looks back to the beginning of the race, especially to man's first attempt to navigate its waters. How the tiny shells were tossed upon its billows. How it can tell of the progress of invention until these white winged birds of commerce began to skim its surface, until man made iron to swim, and these monster steamers, sharp in prow and mighty in wheel, began to people its fastnesses with human beings passing and repassing along great trackless highways, trackless to all eyes save the needle's. Arch polygamist, every ship launched is a new wife added to his harem. Every ship lost is a wife out of favor, given over to the executioner. Miser and highwayman combined, his secret treasure houses are richer than those of Egypt in the days of Joseph. I like him, yet I like him not, and here, with whitecaps breaking everywhere about, I write it down, in his fastness and stronghold of pride and power, I like him not. I rejoice in the vision of Daniel that far as his eye could behold "there was no sea." I thank thee, Daniel, for that touch upon the heavenly canvas. It seals our kinship.

Sabbath on shipboard is perceptibly a different day from the other days of the week. The necessary working of the ship of course goes on, but more of quiet rests everywhere. On the Alaska at 10:30 A. M. the bells toll for service, and all who are thus inclined retire to the main saloon, where the captain, or in his absence the purser, reads prayers. No sermon is allowed, in consequence of past troubles arising from inability to please all parties. In the evening a praise service closes the holy day. Church going people ought to remember more frequently in their prayers those who spend the most of their sabbaths in these wilderness regions.

FRANCIS A. HORTON.

LETTER VII.

CHESTER, ENG., June 8, 1888.

Quaint, charming, ancient Chester, how all our first love awakens again as we walk its narrow streets! Its broken gables, its tiled chimneys, its houses projecting over the sidewalk, its ancient wall, its cathedral, its pleasing suburbs and the like, they greet us as old acquaintances. But why are we here, we whose itinerary requires us to be in a jaunting car on the mountains of Kerry, en route to the lakes of Killarney? Simply because the cold gray mist of Scotland, sweeping down, made it impossible for us to land at Queenstown. Thus for more than an hour we lay off that rough Irish coast in the darkness, and cold and rain blowing for the lighter to come off for those who wished to land. But no one ventured out for us, and when the purser strode into the saloon and announced that the ship would steam on for Liverpool our hearts were lightened of a great burden of fear, and none applauded more heartily than we disappointed ones. We continued to Liverpool, only to find that the same stubborn Scotch adversary had belated us so that we lost the tide and could not cross the bar. This necessitated a sail of fourteen miles in a tug with only a canvas roof over our heads to protect us from the "falling weather" and the rough, cold wind. As one remarked, it was a truly formal English reception, very cold until we become well introduced. Although our tickets read "weather permitting," freeing the company from any obligation to do more than land us at Liverpool, the Guion Company, be it said to their lasting credit, generously offered to send all the disappointed Queenstown passengers back to Cork, or on to Dublin as they preferred. Not being able to spare the time from our work at home to double on our track to reach any place, we accepted an order for a first-class passage to Dublin via Holyhead, and as Chester lies on the line, and as we love Chester, and as we are not specially enamored of Liverpool, what more natural than that we should stop off at this point, and as we have a day or so to spare out of our south of Ireland itinerary, where could we better spend the time than in agreeable Chester? So here we are, and with us seventeen more of the Alaska's passengers, including all but one of the Twilight Club.

Now we must tell you about the Twilight Club, for being only an invited guest at several of their meetings and not a member in full standing, we may be able to say more than a full Twilighter would care to say about their unique organization. The first horror of a sea passage centers in the stomach. That passed and this important member, more obedient than Banquo's ghost, that is to say, being willing to stay down, the next horror centers in the brain, in inactivity resulting in a distressing ennui. And the second works in the interest of the first, for oftentimes something that engages the thoughts leads one to forget the stomach—tides over qualms of squeamishness that would arise if thought were concentrated upon present condition and prospects. Hence good sailors among the passengers are most generally persistent readers. A group of bright, smart folks well known to one another, formed a club whose object was to fight ennui without saying so and, in general, to make the passage agreeable. They gave up the day to hard work in writing poetry, wretched or otherwise, most generally otherwise, with notable exceptions, in conjuring up ghost stories, some of which would make even a ghost blush, in preparing witticisms and other such matters as fertile brains would naturally suggest, and at the hour of twilight they met to read their productions. They had a scribe whose minutes were very witty and were generally disapproved. It was a feast of sparkling wit, of rippling fun, of pleasant railery, knocking out also some truly meritorious productions in prose and verse. This in the rough. We throw it out as a suggestion to intending passengers. If you would be well up in the club tuck away in your satchel the choicest fruits of the scissors for use. If you have any doubts about the most approved method of handling this instrument in such connection call on the city editor of *The Tribune* who will give you full information in his most genial manner.

We crossed from Liverpool to Birkenhead, where we met with

the usual corrections in our English. First, a bright young Congregational clergyman asked the way to the railroad depot, and was met with the reply, "I suppose it is the station you are speaking of?" "Yes," he said faintly, as he began to collapse, "I suppose so." Then another of the party fell into the abyss by referring to the baggage car, and was instructed regarding the luggage van. Then we all laughed again. Next came my turn. I had a through first-class ticket to Dublin and asked whether I should be allowed to lay off at Chester. I was told that I might break at Chester if I wished. Then the laugh was on me. But the climax came when a cultivated lady who, with her charming daughter, has often crossed to this side, and who felt perfectly able to talk baggage in America and luggage in England, told us how she had become confused, and asked the inspector a question concerning her "buggage." The smile broadened into a ripple, the ripple into a laugh, the laugh into a roar, the roar into a haw-haw, in which she took a prominent part. The run down was made in company with one of those genial Englishmen whom we often meet when traveling here, who cannot be at too much pains to tell you every matter of interest as you go along. From him we learned that the rainfall has been entirely insufficient, while the fog has been excessive, so that although everything to the eye is green the ground is dry as dust two inches down. It has since rained and there is a better condition of things. The country is looking very beautiful. We rode out to Eaton Hall, the seat of the Duke of Westminster, and along the roads taken in going and in returning the pasture was deep and tender, the hawthorn, white and red, in bloom, wild flowers everywhere—a most entrancing scene. This duke, by-the-bye, is worthy of mention. His wealth is said to exceed that of any other living man. The gentleman above referred to, born and reared here, stated his income as probably about twenty-five pounds sterling per minute. This dazed me, and after using my pencil for a few moments I got so high in the millions in effort to compute his annual income that I left off figuring. Others hereabouts confirm the same statement. I give it for what it is worth, but I may safely say that His Grace is justified in being somewhat easy in mind concerning his present and prospective financial condition. His landed estate is a paradise, some six miles square, with comfortable homes for his tenantry and household officers and servants. Red and fallow deer, rabbits, pheasants, horses, cows, etc., abound. His celebrated horse, Ben-dorr, cost, it is said, $90,000, but has paid for himself once or twice on the turf. The fee of one shilling, charged to keep out the rabble, admits to his hall, except as to the private apartments. Language, time, and artistic ability fail us to tell of the variety, richness, and beauty of its interior from the mosaic floors of the corridors up to the exquisite wood carving of the ceilings, or of its furnishings. It is like a dazzling dream of fairy land. The hall was originally built two hundred and eight years ago, but has been enlarged and improved from time to time by successive owners. . The Duke owns, also, a large portion of Chester, including the Grosvenor Hall and the Grosvenor hotel, where he is now stopping previous to going to London. He is liberal to the city. In many ways he promotes its interests by a free use of his money, as *e. g.*, building a church at $150,000 cost, and paying out annually £800 for the support of services therein. The wisdom of allowing such money power to amass in the hands of one man under the pro-visions of government is a grave question. It is caste and monopoly combined. At least so it appears to the American mind. But let us not forget that our own problem of government is not yet half wrought out and be sparing of our strictures.

The work of renovating the old cathedral is progressing slowly. When one looks closely to see what is being done the sense of regret passes largely away. The first thought is that they are mak-ing a modern building of one of the grandest of ancient structures. But this is not so. The cathedral dates from the eleventh century. Of course it was built by the Roman Catholics, but when Henry VIII established the Church of England he quickly converted it, with others, to his own ideas. As the centuries passed the interior was whitewashed and the beautiul woodwork was painted. The effort now being made is to remove the whitewash and to restore the anicent appearance of the stone and to paint the mason work afresh. Also the woodwork has been taken down and laboriously treated to remove the vandal paint, a task involving great expense. Thus the effort is to make the edifice more ancient rather than more modern. Dean Howson's grave is in the court, surrounded by grass and flowers. All biblical students look with respect toward the mound under which he lies. To him this work of restoration is mainly due. Dean Darby read morning prayers yesterday in the choir, "and a very poor reader he is, too," said the garulous old verger as full of suggestion as ever. Thirteen choir boys sweetly sang responses and anthems assisted by five heavier voices, one basso very rich and deep. These five were "small guns" of the cathedral, according to the same spiritual authority before quoted, who also added, "the canons reside here only three months in the year." When one leans up against one of these old columns, or hides behind some projection and in the shade falling round him lets the mind take in the thought of seven hundred years, and as with the eyes of this old building sees, and with its ears hears, the happenings of the centuries that lie between, the barbarities and atrocities, the intrigues and jealousies, the superstitions and fanaticisms, the blood-red tide of war bridle deep, the fretted ceiling vanishes, nave and aisles and choir and lady chapel and crypt and chapters and cloisters all become one transporting chariot of thought carrying him back down the troubled yet ever-improving past. History arises and shakes off the dust of the schoolroom, it lives and breathes, it talks to us eye to eye. The consciousness of a past back of us from which we have emerged becomes distinct, our generation as a link in the endless chain, as inheriting the past and endowing the future, our duty to make our impress for good on the race as it moves down to a day when men shall stand by the monuments of our hands and brains and strain their ears to catch the sound of our remote times—all this comes over us, the particular man falls out of view, man only is seen—we thought we were a mountain, we find that we are only a seaside grain, helping to make up the great beach of Humanity upon which the ocean of time forever beats.

Hawarden House and Manor are objects of deep interest to me and to every American as being the home of Gladstone. It is only seven miles out of Chester, and to go to it is one of the pleasant excursions from this town. It is a place full of grand inspiration. The spirit of the man fills it and its visitor if he has any spiritual capacity. Far different from Eaton Hall, not in the same class, it is yet as much above the ordinary home of the people as we are all happy to see the dear old man elevated. Not the grounds, not the buildings, nothing in the trappings and housings here are great and confer their titled, inherited greatness on a man who may himself lack every element of greatness, but the MAN here is greatness and bestows his title to nobility on every leaf and flower and book and pet that he gathers round his home. That title no court nor queen has in keeping nor can bestow, nor can royalty buy and wear it themselves, save in the great court of the universe in exchange for soul worth, mental, spiritual, moral worth. Here sat the great man when in moments of leisure between governmental studies he took our brilliant American infidel between the thumb and forefinger of his massive intellect, and in language most dignified, and in reasoning most clear, rubbed his homogeneous structure into heterogeneous confusion. A view of the man himself makes infidelity look very cheap. See that massive brow, those lines of thought and equipose of judgment that lie deep cut around his eyes and along his forehead, those lines of determination and persistence about his mouth, that spirit of repose and devoutness that covers him like a robe and well fits him to read the Scriptures in the Hawarden Church, of which his son is rector, as he always does when at home among the people who revere him, and the very man himself as a product of the Bible and of the Christian religion is enough to refute all infidel cavils, whether originating on English, French, or German soil and echoed in America, as the penny whistle echoes the blaring trumpet or as the sea shell imitates the thunders of the deep. And when he opens his lips and confesses Christ and declares his personal faith in him as the foundation stone of his life and character, and when we stop to think of his mental qualities as he witnesses to the faith, of his research, of his varied acquirements, of his knowledge of men ancient and modern, his testimony makes the antics of a brilliant but infidel genius, its sacrilegious caricatures, its audacious blasphemies to appear as unreal, as hideous, as ghoulish as the midnight carousals of witches, warlocks, and towzey-tykes on that famous night when "Kirk Alloway seemed all ableez." Noble Christian man, late may he return to heaven, long may he remain on earth, the foremost citizen in the free Republic of God.

In reaction there is health and pleasure. The bow must be unstrung, rest must follow toil, publicity craves retirement. So this great man whose life is spent among the noble loves to seek the simple, quiet ways and places of the common people. We learned of a "Light Cake and Muffin Shop" in town where Mr. and Mrs. Gladstone sometimes go for a quiet lunch. So of course it was quite the thing for us to encourage the light cake and muffin trade. After some search we found the place, and being assured by the ladies in charge that they often served Mr. and Mrs. Gladstone, we sat down and took a note of things. It is on Newgate street, which from housewall to housewall is not more than twenty four feet wide at this point. The shop is down from the street five stone steps, well worn by use ; is not more than fifteen feet wide, and perhaps three times as long as wide. Directly above the lowest step the ceiling falls several feet and continues throughout at this height,which just admits of a tall man passing under erect. To the left of the steps, as one enters, stands a counter, which is covered with muffins and light griddle cakes, cold and ready for sale. The high window in front is supplied also with a shelf of them in view of passers-by. Near by the end of the counter is a chimney furnished with an iron oven, the top of which is very smooth and clean and capable of holding eight cakes at a time. By its side on a three-legged stool is an earthen bowl of several gallons capacity, small at the base and wide at the top and well supplied with white bubbling batter ready for use. A bright fire within the oven indicates that we may give our order as soon as we please. This done, including tea and light cakes hot for two, we sit down at a small table, two feet wide and eight feet long, covered with oilcloth and entirely empty. On either side a long bench without a back, and on either end a short one of the same country school-house pattern. A japanned tray is produced and furnished with a black earthen-ware teapot and the nicest and cleanest of cups and saucers, with a dainty sugar-bowl filled with cubes, and a wee cream-pitcher full to its little brim. Now business begins. The tea is set to draw, a ladle of batter is emptied into a tin cup to measure it accurately and is then poured upon the griddle. Three of these constitute the size of an order. When thoroughly baked one is placed on a hot plate and generously buttered, then another on the top of the first, accurately adjusted and buttered, then with care the third is placed on the others and buttered. Then the fragrant pile is carefully divided with a sharp knife from the center to the circumference into three equal segments, so that we have nine pieces, each a triangle with a circular rim. The whole is placed before you, you pour your tea while waiting for knife and fork. The cakes are growing cool, while their aroma is making you hot. You

•

give a gentle hint, and quickly learn that no knife nor fork is used in eating the cake, the fingers being quite the thing. So you begin by rolling up a segment and take a bite, and find that it works well enough after all. A second installment of three, with a subsequent one of two as a neat finish, proved ample for a lunch, and for all these with two cups of delicious tea each, we pay down the sum of one and six and go on our way rejoicing.

Dear old Matthew Henry, who wrote the best and longest lived commentary on the Old Testament extant, sleeps peacefully here honored by a monument. In the Cathedral sleeps Pierson, whose exposition of the Apostles' Creed will survive until the general demolition. In the Cathedral square lies Howson, whose joint work with Conybeare on the life of St. Paul is matchless. Near St. John Baptist Church are the rooms where DeQuincey wrote his immortal works. Yonder is the old, old house where Keats scratched his screed upon the window pane with his diamond, when chagrined because the clergy refused to dine with him. Here are old stone ornaments in recent years discovered where Cromwell buried them when he broke the walls. They are now being used in repairing it from time to time. The very soil is full of inspiration. Here lives as patron saint the reputed wealthiest man in the world. Here certainly lives, as a townsman, the greatest man of the present generation, take him for all in all. And over all a halo of royalty hangs, for the Prince of Wales, if I mistake not, is Duke of Chester. Fain would we stay and read and think and talk with men whose ancestors carried on the same trade with themselves, perhaps on the same spot, back, back of no one knows where. But we must up and away.

FRANCIS A. HORTON.

LETTER VIII.

ON THE IRISH SEA, June 13, 1888.

We are leaving Ireland, bound for Glasgow and the north country. It is now 10 o'clock at night, but the long tarrying day in these regions of glorious twilight is but just fading quite away. The sea is peacefully rocking us as a crooning nurse quiets a tired child. The new moon has appeared through broken and flying clouds. We have seen it over the right shoulder, and have devoutly turned our money, but it is a rain moon, and we are sorry, for thus far the six weeks of our absence and journeyings have been passed in constant company with Jupiter Pluvius. Everywhere it has rained, until now we are longing for the company of earth-born mortals who have not so many fields to water. But to-night everything is serene and full of thought. The light plays entrancingly upon the waters; the many lower lights are burning, some steadily, some flashing at intervals; the high chimneys of Belfast have dropped out of sight, but yonder looms up in the twilight, silent and grim, old Carrickfergus Castle of high historic renown. Settling down upon the horizon to the south are two dark objects; steamers they are that lay side by side with us in port an hour ago, that sailed out to sea with us, but now part to meet no more. So sailed out into life a merry group that frolicked erstwhile upon the village green, that picnicked merrily with the girls they chose on holidays too far between, and one sails north and one sails west, and some have met with storms and been dismantled, and some have gone down regretted, all widely sundered on the deep sea of active duty. God grant we all who sail to-day may at last tie safely up in blessed ports.

Wife and I are taking a deal of comfort in the consideration that is shown on this side toward dumb creatures, particularly that most serviceable and most abused of them all, the horse. Perhaps we notice it the more as the room we occupied in an hotel at Philadelphia fronted on a street that was used by a street railway. The slipping of the horses on the smooth cobbles, and the rattling of their hoofs as they caught themselves, distressed us by day and awakened us at night. Passing to this side the first thing we noted, a point that repeats itself everywhere we go, is the change in this respect. Large horses and smaller loads is the order. The big Normandy with his great foot and his shaggy fetlock, harnessed in what seems at first sight to be a waste of leather, handled carefully by men who often walk beside the load, moves along briskly, but with no appearance of being distressed or over urged. In Dublin we saw two men with a cart moving along an asphaltum pavement and with a shovel liberally sprinkling coarse sand over the smooth surface. It was raining a little at the time and the street was slippery. Upon inquiry we learned that it was to keep the horses from falling.

Later on we saw the same thing being done by a street tramcar company. In our electric country, where we think in telegraphy and talk in stenography, where we turn night into day and too often forget that all days are not alike, the horses suffer with the men. The servant is not better than his master, and so the master insists upon killing both. We have no use for the Norman, we want horses that can skip. They must be small to stand the racket that would knock a heavy horse to pieces. The same hurry to get through with much work in a short time makes the drays longer. The discrimination is against the poor horse both ways and so our streets are full of pitiable sights; but whether the over-loaded, over-driven men or the horses in the same category are most to be pitied it is hard to say. No one man is to blame for it. Our society is a Jehu, and it drives man and beast so that nations from afar know us by the dust of our wheels. Is it in the nature of things that we shall ever learn wisdom in these matters? It came over me very powerfully last Saturday as we mounted that quaint car of Ireland, the jaunting car, and road out into Phoenix Park about 3 o'clock. This vast pleasure ground and breathing place was alive with people of all classes. Here in one section tennis games prevailed, then farther on cricket matches were in progress, and farther on still the fleet polo ponies and their daring riders were chasing the ball up and down the grounds, while everywhere over the turf ladies and gentlemen were galloping at full speed, or driving along the road-ways, while others were spinning on the fleet bicycle. It is safe to presume that none of these cared to take Sunday for a repetition.

The same rush and jostle for money that kills our men and our horses encroaches on our Sunday, and if cause and effect could be traced, it might be found to be an important factor in many a

4

failure and perhaps embezzlement. The impression made upon any one who breathes in this restful atmosphere is well summed up in the words of the philosopher at my side, who said : " I have learned a lesson ; when I get home I mean to take things more quietly. I see that people who do so get along quite as well as others, live longer, and have a better time all the way through." It is, no doubt, true that Americans are the hard workers of the world. It is equally true that the national countenance is being deeply seamed with lines of anxiety and eagerness and unrest. We act nervously, as though we were hard after something, bound to get it, but not yet in full possession. Here the appearance is rather that of having obtained something, being glad over it, and of getting the best out of one's obtainment.

The jaunting car, by the way, is a lineal descendant of the ancient low back car. We used to sing an Irish ballad when I was a boy about " Peggy in her low back car," but I never had any idea what it meant. Now I find that the low back car was an ancient vehicle, quite the high toned thing in its day, composed of a roller in place of wheels, on which was arranged a platform with a single seat. Modernized, this is the car of to-day. To the uninitiated it is a ride on the ragged edge, a cross between flying and falling from a roof, and if we have a spirited horse and a driver with a fondness for going back and forth over the car tracks and as near to the passing trains as possible, the exercise contains as much of the wild Irishman as one is likely to get on the old sod. But soon one comes to like them and appreciate their exceeding convenience.

While mentioning matters of somewhat minor importance, it will be in order to refer to the mutton chops of these islands. They are among the most delicious of viands. We must sympathize with the Englishman in America who bewails their absence. In size they are as large nearly as the small porterhouse steak. They are cut thick with a liberal supply of fat. They are thoroughly cooked, yet we should regard them as underdone at home. This is a striking peculiarity. They were thus juicy, and in taste there is not the slightest suspicion of wool, while in tenderness they rank with the tenderloin. Remarking these facts to a gentleman, he discoursed somehow thus: "I think that the excellence of our mutton is due to our climate. We have almost constant dampness, we have no scorching heats in summer to dry the pasture, and no piercing colds in winter to pinch the flocks, so that our grass is always abundant and tender and nourishing. The flocks never wander in search of food; indeed, our fields are small, so that there is no opportunity for them to stir about much. They are quiet and contented, and have nothing to do but stand still and grow rapidly. Thus we secure the best conditions, and to these, with a choice breed at the start, I attribute its excellence." Thinking it over, I believe that he has the right of it. But it is too bad that we lack the necessary conditions. In beef they confess our superiority, also in trotting horses; but in mutton and in racers they claim pre-eminence.

Ireland to-day is in full emerald costume, a ride over any of her great railways being a panorama of pleasing change. I do not wonder that her sons and daughters love her ardently. Despite her many troubles, she is prosperous as a whole, and this fact shows the intrinsic wealth of the land. When the long wished for man shall come who can say just what the situation demands for Ireland's highest happiness and prosperity, and when the day shall come on which such policy shall be adopted, she will at once spring forward on the lines of all useful industries and take an honorable place in the United Kingdom. Her poverty-stricken ones appear on all hands, and while those who know them better perhaps explain the case to their own satisfaction, it strikes a stranger most mournfully. Wages are low, and we are told that living is low too. If it is all on a plane with the appearance of such persons on the best streets, it cannot be high. Groups of happy girls, barefooted and with shawls home over their heads are not more mournful in what they suggest of life and discomforts than in the fact that they seem to think nothing of it, regarding it as a finality, while the others accept it for them as a matter of course. Side by side with these are many of the best men and women the world can show. One of these is John Hogg, a flax merchant of Belfast, through whose courtesy a few of us made a most interesting visit to the Brookfield linen works, inspecting every process from the reception of the raw material to the final folding for market. We shall not soon forget his kindness nor lose the mental photograph of his genial face as we took it at our parting at the quay. I would give half a crown for a picture of the group of five noisy newsboys who stood near him guying a lad on the upper deck. When the clock on that interesting day struck twelve, and the Brookfield poured out its 2,500 operatives into

Crumlin road for their forty-five minutes' nooning, it was a literal sea of humanity, representing all ages, from the gray haired sire to the tender child, called a half-timer, from the fact that they work one day and go to school the next at the expense of the company. We found that wages were very low. We were told that living was cheap to correspond. But we fancy it was cheap not from the low price at which they can secure what our American workmen pay more for, but simply because they don't have the same kind nor amount of food and comforts. Our workmen are better dressed, better housed, better fed, and have more spare money for holiday enjoyment and for evening entertainment. No doubt America is the place for the workingman, and whatever tends to disarrange our tariff to his detriment should be frowned upon and voted against by every man of brawn and by every man of sympathetic heart. When we go to the matter of getting ahead in life the rule applies to all classes of commoners. A distinguished Scotch clergyman in the United States told me that he did not care to revisit his native land for fear of being tempted to remain, and that would be so bad for his boys. God bless America! the country for the man who has his own way to make in the world.

We looked in upon the Irish General Assembly now in session at Belfast. This has always been a remarkable body of men. It is small as compared with the Presbyterian Church I represent, but its influence upon Ireland has been and still is very great. Dr. John Hall, of New York, and Dr. John S. McIntosh, of Philadelphia, are contributions of this church to America in later years. Irish wit played all over their discussions of grave topics, and a loud laugh oft repeated was not deemed disorderly. The lobby, too, took a very prominent part in expressing approbation or the reverse of sentiments uttered in the way of stamping and applauding. This is very singular to us across the water. The popular favorites were unmistakably pointed out in this way. The rank and file of the people are intelligent. They freely discuss church questions and appreciate a good point as soon as it is made. They attend these meetings to such numbers that an admission fee is charged in order to prevent going and coming and to insure better order. When a man pays for a thing he wants it. They go to get the arguments, and are silent that they may hear. One dear brother got tangled in his fractions, as many another has done before him. He was eloquently advocating systematic beneficence, and spoke of the growth of the idea in one's own experience where practiced. He cited the case of a friend who began by giving one-tenth of his income, and became so filled with the beauty and power of the system that he was not content to bide there, but went on leaping far beyond those bounds, and finally gave one hundreth. The merciless laugh of the opposition brought him to his senses, and he clambered upon his feet again and hobbled on in pain to a resting place.

The intermediate examinations ordered by the Government are now in progress. A student can prosecute his work under any teacher he may choose, or at any place or at home, provided he can pass creditably these severe examinations. To stimulate exertion to excel, money prizes are given to the best scholars. One young lady of a family where we passed an hour or two took a £60 prize payable in £20 instalments for three years. A poor clergyman had two sons, who were fine students, who paid the entire expenses of their education by the prize money they earned. This money is the result of disestablishment. It went formerly to appointed favorites who drew large salaries and did little or no work; now it is distributed according to merit and placed where it will do some good. Ulster is just now full of glee over the fact that for the third time in the last ten years a student from the Belfast institutions has taken the senior wrangler in the mathematical tripos at Cambridge. The professors are jubilant, especially the man of intricate figures, the people are proud, the newspapers are laudatory and boastful, and the undergraduates are getting ready for a grand torchlight procession in honor of the victor on his return, and the chances are that he will have a ride on the shoulders of enthusiastic fellows.

When we awake the Clyde hammers will be ringing in our ears.

FRANCIS A. HORTON.

LETTER IX.

GLASGOW, June 16, 1888.

Hast ever sailed on Lomond, the beautiful, among the Grampian sentinels that guard enchanted land? Hast ever rambled by the roaring falls of Snaid or galloped through Glen Arklet, along by Arklet Water, or looked into the heaven deep mirror of Katrine and seen clouds floating numberless fathoms down and birds wheeling their flight far under the surface, or coached through bosky dell and wild defile past Achray and Vennachar and frightened the brown hare from his repose along Ben Ledi's heathery moor? No? Then dream of it, cherish it as a sweet thought lighting up your future, count it among the rewards to which hard service shall fairly entitle you. Anticipation will not lay on colors that experience will need to tone down. You cannot anticipate it, it will come upon you from new sides, it will break over you with unexpected wealth, it will assault you where your guards are down and carry away captive your admiration in spite of you. The dream itself will do you good. From childhood I have crossed the sea but always at night when sleep locked up slow plodding facts, and turned loose all fairy fancies. Through labors multiplied and privations manifold the dream led on, a comfort and a stimulant, beneficial always. And now the early dream has been for years a fact accomplished and it is as helpful in remembrance as it was in fancy. Repetition finds the charm unbroken, a ·joy forever. If you have made this round then sure I am you promised the spirit of these solitudes that when you could spare the time you would return and linger and let the soul within you grow big by communing with itself, and with nature, in its wild grandeur, in soft beauty, in variety and extent, as hereabouts displayed. Pluck up heart and hope, all you my young friends of slender means, there is much in this world worth working for, which when it comes to you will be all the sweeter if seasoned with the thought I have earned it for myself. To industry, frugality, perseverance and personal worth all bars to progress are withdrawn.

But the grumbler was there, with his nose in the air. And where is he not, and where was he ever wanted? Who so blind as not to see that the charm, the restfulness, of foreign travel lie in not having things as one has been accustomed to them. When foreign lands

become like our own then we may as well stay at home. Further-
more, he who looks carefully into things generally finds that there is a
good reason why certain courses were adopted, and that there are
equally good reasons why they are not changed. Certain it is his
complaints will never change time-honored customs nor further his
own comfort. The American who comes away here is not discover-
ing a forgotten land that has drifted off on the tide of time into
unfrequented solitudes, outside the current of progress, and it is not
well for him to assume that he has. Wise men fall in with the prevailing order and make no odious comparisons, and enjoyed themselves immensely.

The Glasgow International Exhibition is in full blast, and holds
out the promise of a very hard day's work to the visitor who will
examine its extensive display. The usual catalogue is presented,
with here and there a variation. We may note the department
devoted to the Queen's Jubilee presents. They are numerous but
very disappointing. In themselves they are totally unworthy of so
great an occasion. But we need to look at them only as vessels
that contained a precious wealth of love and loyalty. In these her
heart found richness ; but an outsider generally jumps to the conclusion that so precious a cargo, on so special an errand, would
have been carried in ships of oriental magnificence. But many of
them fall to the level, and not a few fall below the level, of the best
wedding presents that we have seen displayed in Oakland. Others
are costly—some are royal. The boat in which Grace Darling performed her brave acts attracted much attention. I should scarcely
regard it as seaworthy in a moderate gale when compared with
more modern boats. But she won with it imperishable renown.
However, few remember that she was not alone, that her father was
with her and was in command. Nevertheless she was a brave girl
and deserves all the praise that has been lavished upon her. What
a singular thing is renown. How it flees from those who pursue it
for its own sake and comes unbidden to those who never think of
it. And how little we know what work or action is to last forever
and keep us from being forgotten. Most things are improved upon
by the generations succeeding the one which gave them birth, but
some things seem to have been born perfect at the start. Thus,
that Jacquard loom, weaving intricate figures in lace curtains, even
though with much clatter and confusion, has undergone a vast

amount of improving in the application of the Jacquard idea, but the idea is the same now as three hundred years ago, or was it not quite so long? Then, too, the antique manner of ironing and putting a finishing gloss upon linen fabrics by pounding them is still in vogue, and nothing can take its place. It is about all one's hearing is worth to go into that department of the factory, but once in the whole machine consists of a heavy frame supporting a large roller some eighteen inches in diameter, which is heavily padded by being wound round and round with linen cloth. The fabric is made to pass over this roller, when heavy wooden mauls are dropped on it as it passes the center line. These mauls are of hard wood, some four or five inches square and about four feet long. They stand on end side by side, close together, the whole length of the bed roller, and being furnished with a cleat on one side, they are lifted one by one by means of corresponding cleats inserted spirally into a roller properly adjusted and revolving rapidly. Thus they fall with a wave-like motion from end to end, but they fall hard and rebound, and you know when each individual one of the many scores comes down. It is a sort of roar with distinctness. My first thought was that John Chinaman could get all the noise here that his New Year festivities require.

On Saturday night wife and I took a walk on Argyle street, at least we edged, and elbowed, and crowded our way along through more people than we have ever encountered on any street on an ordinary occasion. Almost without an exception they were of the poorer classes, and our hearts pitied them. So many of them were drinking hard, so many of them of both sexes were drunk, so many women coaxing their husbands home, so much brutality and coarseness, so many rags, so many hands outstretched for alms, so many babies in arms, and in such arms, so dirty, so thin, so ragged. "I belong to the upper ten, the upper ten, the upper ten," sings one side of society with laugh and jollity, and "I belong to the lower five, the lower five, the lower five," sings another side through curses and tears with hunger and filth. The upper despises the lower, the lower curses the higher. Rotten potatoes in the cellar mean diphtheria and death in the parlor. These classes that fill the low grounds will make their baleful influence to be felt upon the high grounds when occasion ripens. The devil is prodding them as with hot irons through his inflaming drinks, and one of these days we shall pay the cost of tampering with them. On the other side the gospel is doing what it can, and all that any one is trying to do, to remove the danger. Fourteen years ago the Holy Spirit, through Mr. Moody, swept this city with a mighty revival. He originated the Sunday breakfast for the poor people who never have a hot meal throughout the week. This has grown into a wonderful work, extending from city to city. Last Sunday we went at 2 P. M. to Tent Hall, off Saltmarket street, to attend the children's meeting and see them at their dinner. Making ourselves known, the general manager took us into the regions behind the scenes, into the store-room and into the kitchen. There we saw two circular boilers, each filled to the brim with boiled rice and milk—twenty-six gallons of milk in each, fresh from the country on Sunday morning, ninety pounds of rice by actual weight in each, and also in each precisely twenty-eight pounds of sugar. This was deemed sufficient of this food to supply the day's demands, but that there might be no disappointment to any a surplus quantity stood ready. Beautiful bread cut into suitable portions was supplied in quantity. Having satisfied ourselves hereabouts we went into the main hall, and being seated on the platform, looked on with interest. First a hymn and an earnest prayer by manager and monitors alone. Then the doors were opened, and in came the throng, some fifteen hundred of them, with towzeled heads, ragged garments, three-fourths of the girls with bare feet, many little girls with smaller brother or sister in arms. They were assorted so that the little folks were on the ground floor, those larger on the side elevated seats, and those a little larger in the gallery rows. They sang with a will, and at a signal up went every hand to be inspected, with the promise that any dirty one should be sent to the bathroom at once. The singing was spirited, and responses in prayer were hearty, and attention to the lesson for the day was close. The letters from those who were taking their two weeks in the country at the expense of the mission were read to the delight of the mass. Then came the trucks loaded with cups holding a pint each of rice and milk, and with bread in abundance. These were distributed to each one present, and were eagerly devoured. I can testify from actual taste that the lunch was a success. In the cold weather rich broth is substituted for rice and milk. It was a sight never to be forgotten. Saltmarket street is one of the very lowest in the city, and the influence of this

5

mission is very salutary. I have spoken only of one feature of the work; there are many others. It is supported entirely by voluntary gifts, and they never have lacked means. Thus, on last Sabbath, a gentleman requested the privilege of paying for the dinner, costing about five pounds sterling.

"Those girls behind you are the problem we have to deal with," said my friend. I looked and saw a large band of misses, from twelve to fifteen years of age, who were coarse, showing low origin, and, I infer, seeking low company themselves. This world is bad enough now, but what a place it would be if all of these kind offices, all of these tender sympathies, born of and inspired by the gospel, were withdrawn. No one would care to stay long in it, and those whose circumstances were such that they could stay with some comfort would probably be assisted out of it by less highly favored people. The future problem of the masses is an immense one. It behooves all men of all classes to put away selfishness to plan, and execute in a larger spirit of brotherly kindness.

Stirling and vicinity must ever be a center of attraction to the student of history. It never looked more beautiful than now, amid all the glories of these early summer days. We do not speak of the dirty, noisy town, but of its historic parts and of its rural environments. Barren mountain, wooded hill, fertile plain, sparkling stream, they never were more charming. Sweet-faced Mary is winning her way to the better heart of man as the years roll by. The din of the old strifes has died away; the questions then up are not forward now. We are enjoying the fruits of those struggles, and forgetting all, as we forget and yet remember our own civil strife; we are coming to see more the fact of a beautiful woman, born in perilous times, surrounded by unprincipled people, educated in a false and bigoted system, making the mistakes that might well be looked for in such a case, and at last atoning terribly by the loss of her own head. She was probably the most beautiful woman who ever lived, and the most to be pitied. Her spirit fills all the air hereabouts; we cannot stir without coming upon something that reminds us of her and awakens a new sigh in the heart over her misfortunes. Nor was she alone. Here Douglas fell by the treacherous hand of his sovereign, under whose safe conduct he retired to the old castle. Yonder is the ghouling hill whereon rolled many a noble head that fell under sovereign displeasure. Through what throes and woes

the race has come on to its present state. What horrid old bar-
barians our fathers were. We have little to be proud of as we look
back, and no reason to be discouraged as we look at ourselves and
into the future.

Dumbarton Cathedral yonder is of great interest to me. It is
supposed to be the seat of the ancient Culdees. Yonder on the
Clyde, near Bowling bay, can still be seen the ruins of Douglas
Castle that marks the beginning of the old Roman wall of Hadrian,
north of which even the Roman Empire never extended. In those
wild regions the pure apostolic succession was preserved, together
with the simple worship of the early days, and here, if anywhere in
the world, the boast can be maintained, with valid history at its
back, that unbroken succession from the apostles in ordination and
service can be found among these Culdee Presbyterians. However,
we do not set much store by these things. We leave the alphabet
at the apostles' command, and not stopping with questions such as
that of "the laying on of hands" we strive to "go on unto per-
fection." But the place is interesting and the facts are true.

Very tender and complimentary mention was made in the
churches on Sunday of the departed German Emperor. He is held
in highest esteem for his manly, personal qualities, as well as for his
relations by marriage to the Queen. The map of Europe has
greatly changed since the day when the London papers flamed out
against his betrothal to Victoria. Then they declared that the
Queen was sacrificing her daughter to a poor fellow who could only
hope to pick up a living by services he might render to the Emperor
of Russia. Since that day Germany has gone to the front, and the
poor mendicant dies the Emperor of one of the greatest European
powers and one of the noblest men in Europe. It is quite remarkable
to read how his education was pushed into all departments. Entering the army at ten years of age ; studying language and literature
under the first scholars of the land as tutors ; entering upon army
commissions at the same time that he entered the university; learning to do stable work and all the round of duty required of the
common soldier, that he might know how to sympathize with, and
not overwork, his men ; learning carpentering and bookbinding as
trades; to come into sympathy with the working people of his
Empire, and at every point observing the strictest discipline, on the
old Emperor's motto, that to command one must know how to

obey.   All this made him the idol of the old man's heart, and more than ever it is likely that the son's last severe and hopeless illness hastened the father's departure.   May God keep the new young Emperor and shield him from the mistake of Rehoboam, in choosing counselors as unwise and hotheaded as youth itself is apt to be.

FRANCIS A. HORTON.

LETTER X.

EDINBURGH, June 20th, 1888.

Many tourists make a mistake in not visiting the beautiful northern city of Inverness.   The route to it is very pleasant and the city itself is worthy of attention.   Many persons have not the time, as they think, although three or four days are all that are needed to do it tolerably well.   Others prefer the continent and hasten off there, while not a few think that when they have made the round of the lakes and taken a look at a few of the larger cities, that then Scotland has no more to offer.   Let me say in one word, that he who misses this trip has not seen Scotland.   The tourist leaves Glasgow at seven o'clock in the morning on a swift, comfortable side-wheel steamer and runs down the Clyde to Greenock.   This sail is always attractive.   The great ship-building works are in full view, the docks of three steamer lines in the American trade are passed, beautiful homes on the banks of the narrow river are very near, the historic remains, the celebrated points, the cultivated fields, the busy towns, all pass in review.   Then the run is made through the • Kyles, or narrows, of Butte.   Round the island the ship winds, often being closed in before and behind by high hills, leaving it open to conjecture where the course will open out.   Grand hills rise one behind another, with still others seen through every valley in the background, piled up with an unstinted hand.   Here and there landings are made where merry picnic parties debark, bent on a happy day.   Then the run is made for the opening of the Crinan canal.   This canal was cut across in order to avoid a long and dangerous sail around the Mull of Kintyre.   Upon reaching the canal at Ardishaig a change is made to a cute little steamer of the most approved pattern and thoroughly comfortable, specially built for this canal service. Away she speeds, sometimes embowered in the foilage of the high trees on both banks, sometimes affording an outlook over wide reaches of plain and hillside, ever changing the picture with every bend in the course. The nine miles passed another change puts one again on a larger steamer. Now an arm of the Atlantic ocean is crossed which leaves no one in doubt as to its identity, and presently before us opens up the beautiful bay and quiet city of Oban. The air now is cool, heavy wraps are needed. The traveler is conscious of his progress northward. Here at six o'clock in the afternoon he lands, and some twenty hotels bid for his patronage. Oban is a famous summer resort. A noble wall is built along the entire front of the city, on which is a smooth, broad walk of concrete, called the Esplanade, furnished with seats, while the bay in front is studded with small boats of all descriptions, in charge of skippers ever ready to do you service. The scene is restful, the air is full of health and vigor, the life moving about is very different from that at home. The day has exhausted the tourist's power of admiring, and so he just sits still and looks on. Meantime, directly in front the sun goes down. He watches it sink, throwing celestial radiance upon cloud and water and houses, and over the wild wooded hills beyond, looks at his watch and finds it is 9 o'clock, with at least three hours yet of daylight for those who care to claim it. Rising early, he takes the steamer at 5:45 o'clock, and precisely at the advertised moment she pulls out and heads northward. Yesterday repeats itself to-day, except that the air is now too cool to admit of sitting in the open with comfort, although the sun pours down without an intercepting cloud.

He is now in the wild Highlands. On every side are monuments of the wars of clans. All day long he will sail through the domains of the Campbells, the Camerons, the Mackintoshes, the Frasers, the Monroes, whose ancestors lived mainly by robbing one another, or died fighting deadly battles whenever they met. At the foot of Ben Nevis, Scotland's highest mountain, he takes steamer on the Caledonian canal at 9 o'clock, unless he prefers to stay over at the Lochiel Arms and make the ascent of the mountain. He is now sixty-four miles from Inverness, twenty-four of which are canal and the remainder open lochs. History and poetry come rushing into mind as familiar names are spoken or read. Snow-capped mountains, covered lower down with heather, stand around him.   He draws his tartan a little closer about him as he paces the windy deck.   The broom and whins in full flower light up the banks and fields with their soft yellow blossoms; shaggy, small long-horned cattle and sheep whose faces seem to have been dipped in ink, feed quietly along.   Crofters' cottages and proprietors' mansions dot the hillside or adorn the lawns.   After a day of full enjoyment and of broader ideas he comes in view of Inverness with its highly culti-vated, suburbs, and at 6 o'clock crosses the gang-plank, voting the two days' excursion one never to be forgotten, in no one least thing to be regretted.   The return by rail, of course, can be done in twenty-four hours to London.   Such, in a few words that limp and halt, are some of the soul's experiences on this trip northward.   Let no one omit it who is not driven to do so by dire necessity.

Inverness is a city of 18,000 inhabitants, beautifully situated on rolling ground, with the river Ness running through the center of it, which is spanned by two or more free suspension bridges.   The city is mostly built of stone, and is very solid.   It is the chief distributing center of this wide northern country, and does the banking for a con-siderable territory.   There is nothing of special note for a tourist in the place itself beyond a hundred other towns.   The courthouse and jail are built in the form of a castle and are some fifty years old.   There is a handsome modern cathedral.   There is a most charming walk laid out with care on an island in the Ness, where birds abound and lovers walk, and all is shaded and quiet and rural.   There is a large asylum for the insane, and the mournful fact appears that there are some seven hundred inmates.   They are to a great extent hereditary cases, arising from inter-marriage.   For example, the Island of Lewis is attached to this county.   A gentleman engaged in the tea trade, having amassed a princely fortune, bought the island and became proprietor.   He died, but his wife remains there with her seat at Stornoway as proprietrix.   There are now on the island some 18,000 people who marry freely among their own relatives.   From this island many cases of insanity are brought over to the asylum, I am informed.

This is only one case.   This whole question of what to do with the cotters and surplus crofters is pressing upon public attention.   Possibly all may not know who these people are.   For their sakes justify me against any charge of pedantry if I explain the terms.   A croft is a small bit of a farm, therefore a crofter is a small bit of a farmer. But the land he lives upon belongs to a proprietor, so that a crofter is further pretty much what we mean by a squatter, except that he squats with knowledge of the proprietor and pays rent as long as he stays. He has a very few acres of arable land—say four to seven—which he cultivates. His food is oatmeal, potatoes and fish. He needs but little money, for oatmeal is cheap, his potatoes he is supposed to raise, and he can have all the fish that he chooses to catch. Not having much to do he does not cultivate the habit of doing much, and upon the whole prefers to have his wife do it all. Generally she manages to monopolize the activity of the family. In addition to the arable land, certain sheep range is granted. A whole community clubbing together have one flock to occupy the range. Formerly the arable land was, in common, laid up into sections with the plow. Every man was conscientious in his work, for the sections were distributed by lot after being planted, and he did not know, in case he slighted his work of cultivating, but that he might draw that very section. But now this is done away for the most part. So much for the squatter farmer whose lands might at anytime be taken back by the proprietor and he left to squat somewhere else. It is a miserable life with no outlook.

The cotter is still worse off. He may be a son of the crofter, who has become a man and has married a wife, and has no place to call his home. His father permits him to build a cottage on a corner of his croft, but he must go away to find employment. By-and-by his son gets married, and what is he to do? This question is pressing for solution. Riots have resulted from the distressful condition of affairs. Thousands of acres, say the crofters, are taken up for deer parks and hunting grounds, and a man is of less value than a deer or a sheep or a grouse. God made us and gave us a home here, and he does not mean us to starve to death. So now and then they rise, and with the Bible and regular devotions going on in one part of the camp, a slain deer may be roasting in another. Not long ago so severe an outbreak occurred that troops were called out to quell the disturbance. Certain it is that the poor fellows have sympathy with them. The proprietors, on the other hand, say that the vast deer ranges are of no earthly use for the crofters. They are barren moors, say they, and the need of keep-

ing them up gives employment to many crofters and the money
made out of them is expended in improvements for the general
benefit. However this may be the crofters say that they would like
a chance to try; that they have converted thousands of acres of barren moor upon which they were allowed to settle because it was
barren moor, into productive soil, subject to constantly increased
rentals, with finally a notice to leave. They think that they could
take Winan's immense range in Rossbire for example—Winan, the
American, who owns a straight hundred miles of land and whose son
was reported upon in *The Northern Chronicle* of Inverness yesterday as being a wonderful sportsman. They think that they could put
his land to better use. So one of the rich proprietors is about to set
out for Manitoba in August next to see what opening presents itself
there for the occupancy of the surplus crofter and cotter population.
Thus the only solution to the question now being considered is
emigration, but in case they refuse to emigrate the question will
return more violently than ever. Here, again, the masses loom up
and demand attention to their condition.

I have been traveling for a couple of days with a reporter of an
Inverness paper. It was very pleasant to meet one of the frater-.
nity. I see so much of them at home and find them so agreeable
that I was anxious to know whether the prominent traits that adorn
and magnify the knights of the press in America were as prominent
here. These are supposed to be a sharp nose to pry with, a pencil
that flies, or as malignant critics say, that takes off its " f " when
it flies, and a wing of powerful stroke to span the wide chasms
between the known and reduce all mystery to a dead level of
history. I fancy that wherever found they are brothers born. A
boy was running along the tow-path with a pail of milk and a glass
which he polished on his coat sleeve from time to time in the presence of the passengers who were supposed to use it, and I being
somewhat tired of the dry bread and foreign cookery in general,
thought perhaps the milk would taste like home. I hailed him, and
what did he do but stare and grin. I hailed him again, supposing
that he misunderstood me, when he grinned all the more. Then
my reporter friend spoke to him in awful gibberish, when over went
the pail and up came the brimming glass in a twinkle. I was in
the land of the Gael, and my English was at a discount. This led to
some questions as to his powers of using the Gaelic language. He

replied: "Yes, you understand, I am working on a proprietary journal, and these grumbling crofters hold meetings, the purport of which we ought to know. So, you understand, I slip down and do them up."

Like all reporters, he knows all the clergy. We had three of the local cloth on board. One of them was reading from a white covered book, and the second was laughing until his eyes were tight shut. He went straight up to them and said, "Ah, now, and do I see you reading a white back book?" They made some explanation that there was a funny story in it about a friend, when he turned away and said to me, "That old clerygyman never laughs. He is one of the very solemn order. They read no novels, little else than the Bible, and draw the line at white back books. It does me good to see him merry. If I were to tell my old mother that I saw him laugh she'd not believe me." Another clergyman came and sat down by him and talked pleasantly, and when he was gone he said to me, "That man got married and went on his tour. A gentleman opened the door of the railway carriage where he was, when he waved him off, saying, 'Don't come away in this; I'm a bride.'" Verily they are all alike, and good fellows, too, most of them. Only my friend was lately married and had been to London on his wedding trip. Herein he sets a good example to all of his associates. A thousand good wishes to Ross, of the *Northern Chronicle*, and to his bonny Scotch bride.

But the trip to Inverness is far from being complete in the northward journey. There now remains before the tourist the return by rail which in no wise falls behind that up by steamer. It is a long ride, but not in the least tedious. After a good hearty dinner at the Royal, and a pleasant farewell to the proprietor, Mr. Christie, and a final play with and caress to his beautiful collie, Sable, the tourist takes his seat in the carriage, and at three o'clock is off like the wind via Perth to Edinburgh. For a little time the pull is a hard one, but presently the descent begins, and the train follows hard upon the heels of the engine. There is an exhilarating sense of gliding down hill through the most romantic glens, over beautiful farms, winding among hills covered with verdure, until at Pitlochry the train runs along the edge of a wild ravine where the scenery culminates. At about ten o'clock the train halts at the Waverly station, Edinburgh, and the never-to-be-forgotten tour ends.

6

Of the city of Edinburgh and its famous buildings I shall say nothing, for all the world comes to Edinburgh. All the world admires Edinburgh, and all the world is wise in so doing. No Scotchman dies happily unless he has visited this Mecca of his race. The city is as clean as the marble steps of a Quaker residence in Philadelphia; it is as orderly as a prayer meeting; it is as stiff and prim as a maid of uncertain continuance, a circumstance intended to be highly complimentary to both. Scott's monument still stands forth one of the first in the world; Princes street is as attractive as ever; the Cairngorn pebbles work up as witchingly as ever into jewelry and possess the unrivalled power to render feminine beholders temporarily insane; the clan tartans in plaids and rugs overcome the gentlemen, and the knee breeches and heavy plaid stockings brings to light the callow American. The Cathedral never looked so massive and imposing as to-day from the front windows of the Palace Hotel. Of all these, as well as of Hollyrood and of St. Giles, and of all the rest, men have written and subscribers have read to their full satisfaction. Let it be ours to glean between the rows. Perhaps we may find as much of the true life of the country and of the interesting incident of travel there as elsewhere. Now, for example, I do not remember ever to have read of a disease that attacts tourists frequently. However, I have met the victims often. They seem to be ashamed of it. Nor did I know how badly it takes hold of one until I had an attack myself. I may call it the "Clean strap." It comes on, for example, when a man finds himself in a small city where the pretty things have taken his last half crown and the only bank politely hands back his letter of credit, regretting, etc. Nothing dismayed, he offers currency of the land of the Stars and Stripes in payment of his fare elsewhere, but finds that the booking clerk at the station does not appreciate the American Eagle at his full feather. Then the tourist's feathers begin to droop, and he to wonder what he is to do. Stay he cannot, for that will be deceiving the landlord of his hotel; to walk he is not inclined; to beg he is not accustomed. Happy is the patient if he can convalesce as did a couple I could tell of, who, having emptied all pockets and pooled all issues down to the last copper baubee, found they could manage to squeeze humbly into Edinburgh third class. For evermore, blessed be third-class wagons. Now ask your friend, lately returned, whether I have not him in mind.

FRANCIS A. HORTON.

LETTER XI.

WINDERMERE, June 30, 1888.

The Esk flows sweetly on through the deeply-wooded glen, but Roslyn, the castle of the St. Clairs, is a moldering ruin. The old yew at its side, with seven hundred years of growth, is green from ground to tip, and will no doubt live on for centuries to come. But year by year the tooth of time gnaws into the ancient pile. The mevis returns each season to warble with ravishing sweetness, hidden among its leafy trees or in gorgeous ivy, but no hand rolls back the crumbling tide that is sweeping man's work away. Yet in its day what pride and pomp and power were here. In those times outside of castle walls there was no safety, inside was absolute dictatorship. In kingly state Earl William held his court on this overhanging crag. Dizzy grows the brain as one looks over the bridge of stone, with hip-high coping on each side, by which it is approached, into the Esk one hundred and fifty feet below. Did ever in those wars fierce foemen grapple here and seek to crowd each other over into that horrible abyss? Proud lords waited on Earl William's will to manage his household and to superintend his table and the like. ' Queenly ladies of good degree, seventy-five in number, attended upon the baroness. In this damp, dirty old vault, musty and disgusting, was their bakery, the oven and chimney still seen. Below it, in another musty vault, was the oven for their meats, which were served on vessels of gold and silver. Rude in its material expression, the pride of the heart was full blown then as now. The castle gate has fallen, but the wall on one side and a portion of the arch are still standing. Perhaps the victors Hertford or Monk broke it thus many years ago. The stalls for the chargers to the right of the gate within still stand unroofed, but the keep, the dungeon, is broken and exposes the circular staircase along which the condemned of his lordship went to languish. In proof of the power and pride of the house of St. Clair stands on the premises Roslyn Chapel, the especial gem of ornamented gothic architecture founded by Sir William. It was never completed, only the chancel and part of a transept being built. These are a study both within and without. The great variety of designs is bewildering, there being no duplication in detail. The high vault of the

nave, in shape the pointed arch, is divided into five parts, each
studded with flowers in stone, yet no two divisions are alike. There
are thirteen varieties of the arch in the building. No two foliated
capitals are the same. The twelve pedestals on which once stood
the apostles are each of separate design. The profusion of ex-
quisite stone carving about the altar is great. The three columns
in front of what now is the altar, but which was intended originally
for confessional boxes, are unlike. One is wound with pomegranate
without fruit; another is fluted; the third is a pattern figure. Of
course it was all done for pride and piety combined. The barons
were all buried under the floor; old Sir William, without coffin or
shroud, was laid down in full armor. Walter Scott has immortalized
the chapel; and Drummond, whose home was hard by in this same
glen of the Esk, has sung its praises. One can well see how the
minstrel's soul would swell and his hand would grasp his harp,
or pen, as he sat amid these surroundings and let the past roll over
him. Musty old stone heaps, they need a soul in the beholder to
interpret them; then they grow young again, and full of deepest
interest.

Come with me, ye who love to dream of the past (and who with
a soul does not), and let us go for a day-dream up into the castle
here in Edinburgh. Roslyn out yonder on the Esk, seven miles
from town, is of yesterday beside the antiquity with which we shall
surround ourselves. That cannot go beyond the eleventh century.
This no man can get behind, it is lost in antiquity. Here then is a
range for imagination's mightiest wing. Get up and lean against
Mons Meg, the famous cannon, made of bars of malleable iron running longitudinally with rings of the same material, sprung on, and
dating back at least four hundred years. Thus we are leaning
against Old Antiquity to start with. America drops out of sight as
we look at Meg. When she first spoke Columbus was begging
ships to hunt for bigger countries than he had in mind. Glance
over Meg and let the eye fall on St. Margaret's Chapel, then Meg
falls out of sight. One thousand and eighty A. D. What a leap!
Eight hundred years backward from to-day; and those walls in part
and that interior arch complete of carved stone, have stood through
all these centuries and have watched the pen of history making its
long-drawn records. Back of this chapel, in its place in time,
comes the record of the considerable town of Edinburgh as early as

eight hundred and fifty-four. Back of the town in time was, of course, the original castle stronghold, no doubt correctly asserted to reach into the period of the Saxon heptarchy. It was only as people dared to venture that cities grew up around the strongholds. The old Greeks had their Acropolis, with houses about the foot from which the people could run into the strong tower when danger threatened. The writer of the Proverbs makes the same references. Thus out of the dim past, and following its ideas, we see arising this ancient castle, on the top of this inaccessible hill, beyond the reach of catapult or battering ram, and a sheer thousand years above the date of gunpowder. By time, by fire, by vandal hand, the old has dropped piecemeal away, the new has come into its place, the location ever the same, the identity preserved, but changing in detail. We see it in its loneliness—grim, threatening, in that early morning of the Christian era. The air is chill with cruelty, lawlessness, and rapine. There was no safety within the range of jealousy, below it there was none save in vassal submission. Time rolls, manners soften, and law grows respectable, then the castle gates open and the city begins to grow on Castle Hill. Then on comes Holyrood yonder, with the ruined abbey, whose roof has been down for fully two hundred years. Then about Canongate the city grew. Little by little we unroll the map and see the city expand under our eye. Finally the valley is passed and the new city comes in, until now about this mother castle, whose "top is bald with dry antiquity," the daughter city lies 200,000 strong. And what men and women her census has enrolled. What warriors, what statesmen, what jurists, what preachers, what reformers, what scholars and writers. There is more brain in Scotland's soil than the combined world has in action to-day. What martyr blood has drenched her acreage; what beasts like Claverhouse and bloody Mackenzie have ravined among her chosen ; what horrors of cruelty have been performed. Let us arrest the dream, it will end in nightmare, and we shall start affrighted as though we heard the hoofs of Claverhouse's troopers and saw the black "Maiden" embracing us with her long arms and dropping her sharp blade to kiss our necks. To drink in these inspirations, to cause the edges of our historic ideas to become clean cut, to provoke to more full and careful study, are some of the advantages of travel. Parents who can afford it can do no better thing for their studious children than spend an

occasional vacation in this sort of object teaching   For the lazy
boys and girls, of course, let no provision be made.

What loss the world would sustain were all its ancient church-
yards done away.   To many they contain nothing but bones and
stones and unpleasant reminders.   But to those who take in human
life in its fullness, as continuing beyond the tomb (the best of it
lying beyond to those who live best here), it becomes a vast picture
gallery, only in the reverse order of the usual experience, for in
them we have the paintings without the catalogue, but here we have
the catalogue, and memory or biography must needs supply the
likeness.   In the midst of the roar of life about Parliament House
square, Edinburgh, when one stumbles on that iron brick in the
pavement, about eighteen inches square, inscribed simply with two
raised capitals, I. K., and realizes that underneath lies the bones of
John Knox, the vision springs forth at once of that man of whom
Regent Morton said he never feared the face of clay of that faithful
witness who minced not the truth even for the sake of Mary ; who
preached with such soul intensity that one of his hearers said it
seemed as though he would dash his pulpit "a' to blads"; who
loved Scotland so that in his prayer he cried to God, " Give me
Scotland or I die !"   To read these facts is one thing, but to come
in contact with the very places that knew them last is far another.

Grey Friars is replete with blood-curdling history.   No picture
gallery in Europe can so stir the soul.   Westminster Abbey is alive
with the most distinguished company to be found on earth.   Let us
adhere to the sweet, natural method of caring for our bodies when
the soul lays them down as no longer needed.   The contrast of this
has been haunting me for days, ever since I examined at Glasgow,
in the Bombay department of the exhibition, the Indian Tower of
Silence.   I have wondered whether I ought to write to you about it,
but it seems to come in properly just here.   It consists of a very
high wall in the form of a circle, having a very considerable diameter, all, of course, open to the heavens.   About half way up on one
side the wall is pierced for a doorway that is reached by steps.   No
one enters the tower save the dead and those who minister to them.
At the foot of the stairs all relatives take final leave and turn away.
The door opens upon an inclined floor, sloping toward the center and
terminating in a circular well of large size.   Side by side, as closely
as they can be cut in the stone floor, all around next to the wall, with

their feet pointing toward the well, are excavations large enough to hold a full-grown man, and a few inches deep, with a valley cut from the foot emptying into a drain that runs to the well. Inside these a circle of the same number, but smaller in size, graduated according to the narrowing circle for the bodies of women, and inside these, close around the well, a row of the smallest size for children. When a body is received it is stripped entirely naked according to the word, "Naked came I into the world and naked shall I go out of it," and laid in one of these receptacles. In a few hours the vultures, which hover about this feeding ground, have removed every particle of flesh, and the tropical sun and rains finish the work. The bones are then thrown into the well—king and peasant alike, rich and poor, according to the word, "They shall lie down alike in the dust." Three openings lead from the well by means of drains to the outer soil. The whole conception is horrible in the extreme, and is one of the outgrowths of heathenism. Earth and fire being sacred, the body may neither be buried nor burned, for in so doing these holy elements would be polluted. The more widely we look abroad on the earth the more we find reason to be thankful for our home in Christian America, and the less we are inclined to copy the manners and customs of antiquity. The world is growing better every day. Let our faces be toward the future and not toward the past.

We have been rambling through the home of Walter Scott at Abbottsford on the Tweed. What a modern pre-Raphælite he was. How he wrought to the last degree of faithfulness. I have seen artists of this school at work. Every leaf had to be an exact copy of the leaf before the eye. A leaf was not a leaf to them—it must be this leaf, and the tendril must have the exact number of curls, etc. One of them had all of his furniture made by a joiner at great expense that there might be no seeming but all reality, the tenons must pass through the mortices, not go half way through with a cap on the other side to simulate, and so forth. So Sir Walter seemed to work. He put himself in contact with the things he was writing about and he was faithful to nature. Hence the origin of his armory full of all queer, quaint, interesting, rare, and horrid things. When he wanted to describe an old gun, or pike, or key, or thumb-screw, he took the article down, and like the artist with his leaf and tendril he described it exactly and minutely. This is a charming idea, yet one whose execution calls for patient and pains-taking labor. In literature such men make sure of their facts, not in the main but in the fractions; in theology they deal with exact statements. And the result in every case is work that must and will abide. His love for Roslyn Chapel and Melrose Abbey is seen in the very many copies he has made from them in the wood carving of his house. The grotesque figureheads were reproduced in ceiling and corbel in great numbers. He stands high in Scotland both literally and figuratively. The latter in every mind and heart, the former in St. George's square, Glasgow, where he surmounts an elevated shaft, while far down below him on one side is an equestrian statue of the Queen, and on the other side is an equestrian statue of the Prince Imperial Consort. Thus at the last reckoning intellect is king, while prince, queen and people gladly do it homage.

Leaving Melrose we turned aside into the wonderful lakeland of England, the most charming of all places in the kingdom. Mountains standing round on every side, of course, make valleys and in these lakes have formed in great number with lovely, quiet, recesses suitable for study and meditation, or for rest to a tired brain. At Keswick we come upon Southey. Around Windermere we find the walks of Wordsworth; we see the fields through which he tramped, crooning aloud some new poem as he shaped and reshaped it in his mind, which the farmers described as his "booing to himself" as he walked along. There is a path to a rock on the shores of the lake. Climb it and you will see it is the poet's idea of its chiefest point of beauty. Here, too, is the house of Harriet Martineau, like all the others built of cold-gray stone. Here lived and died Hartley Coleridge in the old house by the way. Up that glen is the residence of Doctor Arnold, late master of Rugby. No wonder they came to settle here. The quiet that literary people love, the close heart contact with nature, the cliffs to challenge a climber's muscle, the woodland to evoke thought, the waters for dreamy, floating and reverie, all are here, and the birds, oh! the wonderful birds, the thrush singing like the leader of nature's choir; the lark, heaven high, sending melody down, they, too, are here. No wonder that a lover of birds whom I know wished she had a cage as big as a forest and had them all in it with barrels and barrels of cracked wheat to make them evermore happy. Most heartily do I commend this lake region to solicitous wives who see their husbands running down and the day nearing when they must perforce go away somewhere. You cannot go amiss of a quiet home in an hotel, or in more private apartments, if desired. The whole region is given up to entertaining guests from abroad. Coaches with four-in-hand run daily at various hours between Bowness and Keswick, through Windermere, Grasmere, Ambleside, Rydal, and other villages, while side excursions can be made in the same way to Buttermere, to see how the waters come down from Lodore, and to other points of interest. Heavy shoes, loose, easy flannel sack coat and trousers, and an equally simple rig for the ladies, does for the most of the time, or a tennis suit, if you play, will answer, and no criticism will be passed upon you by any one. You come to rest, and you get what you come for.

The architecture of these islands might be greatly improved by some of our American architects. Its prevailing characteristic is heaviness and coldness. These elegant lawns and charming nooks and sightly knolls offer a premium for a tasteful, bright, cheery house. But they are not met with. Now and then some one breaks rank as far as he dares, and the change is welcome to an American accustomed to the prettiest cottages and mansions in the world. In Edinburgh, for example, the sensation is that of walking in a chilly corridor. The streets are paved with stone blocks, the sidewalks are stone, the front porches are stone, the walls are stone, and all of one color, from the center of the street to the top of the house. The doors are massive and cold, and dignified with their polished brass knockers and plates; there is nothing to warm them up. Here and there a red curtain over the front door, in place of the usual plaster figure, and red curtains at the window impart warmth, so that one draws near to such a house instinctively. Here in this charming district, which by its very character calls for pretty girls with white dresses and colored sashes, with all that beautiful variety of cottage that can be found on the New Jersey coast or in California, the houses are all stone, slatestone at that, of all uneven widths, laid up in mortar, but the mortar is so far in as not to appear to the casual observer, giving an appearance of haste and instability, like a stone fence about a sheep pasture.

In fact, take it all through, we think America a good place to live, while enjoying the old countries for a time. Said a well-traveled

7

Englishman on a coach to us: "You do make awfully good cakes in America." "What kind?" was the reply. "Oh! five or six kinds; I could eat a whole one now." "And," he went on to say, "you do have a great many handsome women in America." We assented, of course, and thought more than we cared to express. The delicacy, refinement, and general attractiveness of our American ladies are not easily duplicated in any land we have gone through.

Hotel registers begin to show more of the names of delegates to the Pan Presbyterian Council as we get nearer to the great city where the meeting is to be held that called us over. We hope to be as diligent in the hard work upon us there as in filling in this enforced period of waiting. After that is over we shall hasten home via Bremen, passing through the great and attractive cities on the way. The good ship Eider will carry us safely through, we trust.

Francis A. Horton.

Letter XII.

London, July 11, 1888.

How shall I write to you about the great Pan Presbyterian Council? Shall I give you the actual facts and be regarded possibly as boasting, or shall I suppress them and go roundabout the subjects, giving incidents and impressions, thus feeding you with the manna that falls round about the camp? I cannot believe that you desire less than the facts, and I can easily believe that all will rejoice with us in the mighty power and wide reach that we have secured among the nations of the earth for the cause of truth and righteousness. I had no idea of the state of the case myself, and I am sure that others less intimately associated with our faith and order will be even more surprised than I.

With indefatigable labor Rev. G. D. Matthews, D.D., of Quebec, Canada, convener of the Committee on Statistics for the Council, has collected and arranged a mass of facts and figures, filling 300 printed pages. These are reliable data on Presbyterian matters, and the only full and orderly compilation extant. Of course, therefore, it is an exceedingly valuable book to any man interested in statistics, and can be procured by addressing him as above and remitting one shilling—*i. e.*, twenty-four cents—and about six cents more for postage. Speaking by this book, as well as by the roll of this present council, which we have heard called and responded to by the living delegates, there are representatives of twenty-six organized church bodies holding the Presbyterian system on the European continent. These comprise 383 presbyteries or classes, with 4,844 pastoral charges and over 470,000 communicants. The wide diffusion is quite remarkable, and to me was a genuine surprise. They are found in Austria, Bohemia, Moravia, Hungary, Belgium, France, Germany, Hanover, Greece, Italy, the Netherlands, Friesland, Poland, Lithuania, Spain, and Switzerland.

Passing to the United Kingdom, we have twelve organized bodies, giving a total of presbyteries in the British churches in England, Ireland, Scotland, and Wales of 292, with over 5,000 pastoral charges and more than 1,250,000 communicants. Passing to Asia, we have three organized bodies in Persia, Japan, and Ceylon, having ten presbyteries, 126 pastoral charges and over 10,000 communicants. Passing to Africa, we have eight organized bodies, with sixteen presbyteries, 223 pastoral charges and over 54,000 communicants. Passing to America, we call the roll of eighteen organized bodies with 653 presbyteries or classes, 14,893 pastoral charges, and 1,562,000 communicants. These are all in Canada and the United States. Passing on to Australia we enumerate eight organized bodies with forty presbyteries, 1,142 separate congregations, and 31,639 communicants. Passing on to New Zealand we have two organized bodies, with thirteen presbyteries, 481 separate congregations, and 18,622 communicants. Passing on to the West Indies we have one organized body, the Presbyterian Church of Jamaica, with four presbyteries, forty-six pastoral charges and 8,977 communicants. To sum it up we enroll 78 organized bodies, with 1,392 presbyteries, 25,689 pastoral charges, 27,996 separate congregations, 3,448,225 communicants, and 2,879,721 Sunday school attendance.

It will be noticed that, take the world around, the number of communicants is in excess of the number of Sunday school attendants by over half a million. In the American churches the communicants are 1,562,000, and the Sunday school attendance is 1,446,390. It will be interesting to know whether this fact holds true in the case of each of the other bodies, and it will be profitable to discuss the question whether this is giving a good account of all the children in our land. In addition to these organized bodies there is a very long roll of what are called the *Diaspora*, or dispersed churches. We have been so much under the harrow of persecution that the seed has been scattered and covered under in many of the out of the way places of the earth. In all the lands named, and in almost every land that can be named, are separate congregations of Presbyterians provided with place of worship and pastor. Hundreds of such have reported to the Alliance, which is the only body with which they have any connection, and through which they will be brought into the closest sympathy and co-operation with the great body. The final estimate of the numbers of our order on the face of the earth is above 4,000,000 of communicants, and not less than 20,000,000 of adherents.

To sit in council with brethren thus gathered together from the ends of the earth, to look into their faces and note the strong national traits; to hear them speak, either in their own tongues or in broken English, and utter the same sentiments and declare the same experiences common to Presbyterians everywhere, is like the sitting down in our Father's kingdom, where all who love the Lord Jesus in sincerity, from every land and of every name, shall come home, the organized bodies and the men and women of the dispersion who, for various reasons, have not joined any church body, but are for all that the Master's; all declaring one great love to Him who loved and died for all. Here it is the man speaking and the sentiments expressed that are considered, with not one thought of what end of the earth he comes from, nor with what body he stands connected. How like that which is in store for us by and by.

I knew, of course, that wherever our church goes she fosters education, but the array of our literary institutions upon earth is imposing beyond my expectation. Pass our colleges and literary schools and note particularly the list of theological seminaries. Beginning with Austria we have the Imperial Royal Evangelical Theological Faculty in the University of Vienna, consisting of six professors maintained by the State. In Hungary we have the College at Saros Patak, with seven professors, who claim to lead in all free inquiry and liberal ideas; the College of Debreczen, dating back to the Reformation, having 725 students and ten professors in the theological faculty; the College of Nagy-Enyed with six theological professors; the Academy of Papa with six theological professors; and the Academy of Buda-Pesth with the same number of men in the theological faculty. Well done for Hungary. In France we have "the Faculty of Protestant Theology" in the University of France, the nine professors of which are appointed by the State on nomination by the reformed churches; also we have the theological faculty of the Academy of Toulouse. In Germany we have one chair in the Kaiser William University, Strasburg. In the Netherlands we have two professors always in the University of Leyden, in which faculty is also the celebrated Kuenen, one of the foremost critics of the rationalistic school. Professors Goozen and Offerhaus are the present appointees of the Dutch Reformed Church. Also in the University of Groningen we have two theological chairs, and all the faculty have perfect liberty of teaching. In the University of Amsterdam we have two chairs in the theological faculty. The Free University of Amsterdam is ours exclusively, being a protest against the infidelity that appears in the National Universities. In 1854 was founded the theological school at Kampen, which has now eighty-one students in attendance. In Italy the Waldensian Church comes out of the fires of its terrible persecutions, which were never able to bring it into connection with Rome. Presbyterian always, from the apostles down, with its theological seminary which in 1860 was removed from Torrepellice to Florence and the Free Church has its Theological Hall at Rome, of which grand old Father Gavazzi is head.* Many of your readers will remember him, as he has spoken in our churches. In Spain the Reformed Church has its theological college at Cadiz under charge of the Presbytery of Andalusia. In Switzerland, at the Universities of Bale, Zurich, and Berne, in addition to the ordinary theological faculty, are in each case a number of what are called private docente, each of whom is a member of the Reformed Church. The Free Church has at Lansanue a theological faculty of three professors with J. Frederic Astie at the head, and at Neuchatel the Evangelical and Free Church; each has a theological seminary. So also at Geneva, each of these churches has its school of theology. In England there is but one, on Guilford street, London. In Ireland there are three, two at Belfast and Magee College at Londonderry. In Scotland there are nine—of the Established Church: St. Andrew's, Glasgow University, Aberdeen University, and Edin-

---

* Father Gavazzi has recently died.

burgh University; of the Free Church: New College, Edinburgh; Free College, Aberdeen; and Free College, Glasgow; of the United Presbyterian Church: Theological Hall, Edinburgh; and of the Secession Church, Divinity Hall, Glasgow. In South Wales is Trevecca College. In dark Africa we have a theological Seminary at Cairo, with three professors and fifty-six students; also one at Stellenbosch, Cape Colony; and another at Burghersdorp, Cape Colony. In America we have of the Northern Church, Princeton, Auburn, Alleghany, Lane at Cincinnati, Union at New York, Danville in Kentucky, McCormick at Chicago, San Francisco, German at Dubuque, German at Newark, N. J., Lincoln University, Pa., and Biddle University, N. C. The Southern Church has Union at Hampden, Sidney, Va., Columbia, S. C., Austin, Tex., and Tuscaloosa, Ala. The Reformed Church has New Brunswick, N. J., and Hope College, Mich. The Reformed Church in America has Grand Rapids, Mich.; the German Reformed has Lancaster, Pa., Heidelberg at Tiffin, O , Ursinus at Collegeville, Pa., and Sheboygan, Wis. The United Presbyterians have Xenia, O , Newburg, N. Y., and Alleghany, Pa. The Associate Reformed has Due West, S. C. The Reformed Presbyterian has one at Philadelphia, Pa., and the Cumberland Church one at Lebanon, Tenn. Canada shows us Queens at Kingston, Ont., Knox at Toronto, Halifax, Morvin at Quebec, Montreal, and Manitoba at Winnipeg. In Australia we find St. Andrews at Sydney, Ormond at Melbourne, Divinity Hall, Brisbane, and Union in South Australia. In far off New Zealand we find the University of New Zealand and the College of Dunedin. In the West Indies the seminary at Kingston, Ja. In Asia we have the theological school at Beirout. In Persia the Seminary of Oroomiah, and others like these two last on mission fields to the number of thirty additional, which I will not weary you by naming.

To sum up all we have scattered over the world, eighty-seven theological seminaries with 347 professors, 3,624 students, and 892,-657 volumes in their libraries. Surely all will rejoice with us that we belt the round globe with schools of investigation into truth, raising up men to defend and proclaim the faith once delivered to the saints. Coming up from all these different and widely separated centers where they have pursued their independent studies, there is much of divergence of view on many points. There is many a grapple and tug, but in and through all there is one ring and accent that proclaims the family to which all alike belong.

I shall not weary you with extending statistics, but shall do my subject injustice in the sight of all Christian workers if I do not give a few hints at what this vast body is doing. In point of money contributed for purely religious work within denominational bounds, the figures will not fall under $10,000,000 for the last year. The various Woman's Boards of Missions alone gave over £100,000. In the field of foreign mission we are sustaining 521 foreign and 349 native ordained ministers, with 281 licentiates; and other agents, 575 foreign and 3,702 native—a total for the Presbyterian Church of the world of 5,248 persons. The adherents on mission fields to our churches are 284,146, all baptized, of whom 56,419 are communicants, about as many as the population of Oakland. We have also on these fields 1,728 boarding and day schools, with 84,752 scholars under instruction. The purely denominational religious papers and periodicals of the church number 284. But enough in the department of statistics. In the matter of woman's work, it is enough to say that among the many organizations named none makes a better showing nor receives more commendations than our own Occidental Board of the Pacific Coast.

This, in short, is the body lying back of this council, and now the appropriateness of the name assumed by it is clearly seen, viz.: The Alliance of Reformed Churches Throughout the World Holding the Presbyterian System. Now also its character is clearly seen. It is merely an alliance, with no power except to confer together on vital questions that concern the church and the common faith. In debate the utmost freedom is allowed, the most advanced ideas being presented, and when printed are understood to be individual opinions, the alliance not being committed thereto. The Christian religion has nothing to fear from the unfolding of truth, and the Presbyterian Church is in the front ranks of those who search for the truth in every open field. The comparison of notes upon methods of work is also of great value, especially to those who are in a large measure isolated, and to those who live in lands that are not so forward and active in all these matters. It also tends to repress too great activity where by surroundings men have been led on to ultra and, upon the whole, exceptional practices. Scotland is a balance wheel upon America and America is a stimulant for Scotland. Also measures of great moment can be carried by this concerted action, *e. g.*, co-operation in foreign mission fields has received an impetus in this council that will impel all Presbyterian churches far in that most desirable direction. When the bodies are thus eye to eye suggesting, amending, asking and replying, proposing and discussing, the ends desired are furthered rapidly.

This is the body, and for such purposes assembled, that is now holding its closing sessions in this city. I will not pretend to call the roll of the great and well-known names in church and state, in the pulpit and in the sanctum, who sit daily here in conference. But to see the men I long have known by reputation, to talk with them, to hear them speak on vital questions, is one of the events of my life. It will be of lasting benefit to me personally, and to my work in its further prosecution. I only wish that all of my friends might enjoy the feast with us. In my next letter, which will probably be my last, unless I find something in the celebration of the Fourth of July in Paris, or in the sewers of that beautiful city, to write about, I will give you a running account of events from day to day. In this I have aimed to make you acquainted with the body itself that stands at the head of world-wide Presbyterianism.

It was my honor on last Sabbath to be selected to preach for the people of London's most celebrated man of our order, Rev. Donald Fraser, author and pulpit orator. He is a tall, slender man, with a mass of snow white hair covering his head and with white side whiskers. In action he is dramatic, in language he is limpid and forcible. The hem and the haw and the drawl of ordinary British oratory disappear in him ·as in Gladstone. His church is plain without, but quite beautiful within. The pulpit is high and white, with staircase in the rear by which it is entered; which done, a church officer draws a red plush curtain behind the preacher and he · finds himself nearly on a level with the gallery. Of course, I wore the plain black Genevan gown to which the Presbyterian Church in the older countries and in many parts of America has always adhered. It was a great mistake for any to depart from the custom, for several reasons, which we will not stop to mention.

Coming down at the close of the service, who should appear before me but Trustee Dalziel of my church, of the firm of Dalziel & Moller, Oakland, California. It seemed like a breath from California. Then came Miss Haight, also of my church, who has been on this side of the ocean for about a year. Wherever we go we find Californians. Also we find enthusiastic friends of California. Last night we dined at Hampstead, London's most beautiful quarter, with Mr. Edwards, who visited us last year, in company with Rev. John Dunlap and Rev. Mr. Matthews, in the interest of Christian work among the Jews. He is brim full yet of the visit, is booming California, and like all others who have ever undertaken to say much about it, is not believed. He says that he only wants a reasonable excuse for so doing, when he shall at once repeat his visit. During a walk of three miles around Hampstead heath, looking from those heights down upon London, lying on all sides as far and farther than we could see, with St. Paul's looming up above everything, and revealing its greatness as it does not from a nearer view, he talked America in all the intervals of local description. Miss Josie Simon is here with her mother, cultivating her wonderful voice. She has sent me her card, and I hope to call upon them before leaving for home via Paris and Bremen.

FRANCIS A. HORTON.

LETTER XIII.

LONDON, July 12, 1888.

At eleven o'clock on Thursday morning, July 3d, the fourth meeting of the Alliance Pan Presbyterian was called to order in Regent Square Church, this city. The first council was held at Edinburgh, at which the late Rev. Dr. Eells, then pastor of the First Presbyterian Church of Oakland, was present as a delegate. Four years later the second council was held at Philadelphia, Pennsylvania. Four years later the third council was held at Belfast, when Rev. Dr. Sprecher of Calvary Church, San Francisco, formerly of Oakland, was the Pacific coast delegate. This year it is in London, and the First Church of Oakland is again in honor, having for the third time a pastor in representation. Four years hence the council will be held in Toronto, Canada. One other church came under my notice that had three pastors present in this one council; that was the First Reformed Dutch Church of

8

Catskill, New York, Rev. Dr. Welch, professor in Auburn Seminary, your correspondent, and Rev. Dr. Van Slyke, the present incumbent.

Regent Square Church is memorable as being formerly in charge of the late Edward Irving, who went out from us and founded the order of Irvingites, named for him. Those whom I have met of his followers are men and women of pure life and noble purpose. While not accepting his doctrines, we raise no question as to his motives and speak a good word for his followers.

The devotional part of the services was led by ex-Moderator Smith of the Northern Church of the United States, the small, cramped pulpit admitting of but one occupant at a time. When he came down, the pastor of the church, Rev. J. Oswald Dykes, who is also at the head of the Presbyterian College of London, went up and preached the opening sermon. Principal Dykes is a comparatively young man, of stalwart frame, with a clear mind and choice use of language. The sermon was not in the least bigoted, but broad, charitable, yet laying again the grand principles which, from the Reformation onward, have borne the weight of the reformed churches. This over, the concluding prayer was offered by Rev. Dr. Monod of Paris, whose English is very pure, and whose presence on the rostrum all through the council was a signal for applause. He is a small man with dark complexion, deep set black eyes, long, jet black hair, a lock of which persists in falling into his right eye. He has a great soul, and it is all on fire with the work he has in hand for the Master. Then Dr. Dykes constituted the council formally with prayer, in which he remembered the heads of the various lands represented—Queen Victoria first and President Cleveland next.

Then came the roll-call of the three hundred delegates. Every ear and eye of the vast audience was at its best to catch the name and to recognize the man it represented. To aid in this the delegates were requested both to respond and to rise in their places. It seemed like an echo from the last great roll call of the future, and I fancied this eagerness to see men of whom we had long heard and by whose books and writings we have been instructed in many things, was not unlike the interest you and I will take in detecting Moses and Paul, Luther and Knox, Wesley and Whitefield, and many others on that great day of assembling. The usual custom was followed of having a new presiding officer at each session, and the aged Rev. Dr. Cairns was placed first in the chair. He is admitted to carry as much of the brain of Scotland as any other man now living. He is very large and has white hair and beard and is of commanding appearance. The organization completed and the hour of adjournment having arrived the evening session was omitted in order to enable the delegates to attend a reception tendered to them at Argyle Lodge, Campden Hill, the town residence of the Duke, the MacCallum More. This was the first of a series in which the London Presbyterians endeavored to equal the hospitality of the cities that had previously entertained the council.

Manifest difficulties were in their way, growing out of the immense London distances scattering widely the members of the churches, but, despite all, they succeeded in doing admirably, beginning with this reception by the Duke of Argyle and ending with one by the Earl and Countess of Aberdeen. I may as well speak of them all in a lump and not refer to them again. A long underground ride brought us to the station, a short walk brought us to the lodge, where we were received by Lord Balfour of Burleigh, the duke being detained at the Lord's by an important debate that was on. The beautiful lawns were at the disposal of the guests—in one place a large tent for speaking, and on either side of it two smaller tents with refreshments. A band furnished music of one kind and a company of pipers music of another sort. The last was the more unusual and therefore most interesting, albeit their music was good. Speeches in due time were made by men from Canada, United States, England, Ireland, France, and Hungary. Dr. Lynd spoke for Ireland in a very witty address, claiming for Ireland every good thing that has gone out into the world. Evidently the blarney stone has spread its influence to the far north in the Emerald Isle. The refreshments were ample and excellent, the young ladies behind the tables doing the honors wore uniform apparel and looked very pretty. The only drawback, at least to us who do mind such things, was the fitful rain, pouring madly at one moment and the sun smiling the next, as though to see how much of this we could stand and not get out of humor. For three days the entire body of delegates and some of their elect ladies were lunched at the New Holborn restaurant in fine style after the morning session, which ended at three o'clock. This was an expensive piece of entertainment. Then on Saturday two excursions were planned, one to Cambridge University and one to Hampton Court and Kew Gardens, the choice being given.

We chose Hampton and Kew, and with a train load visited those interesting places, under guidance of a gentleman thoroughly informed in all the details of history centering in the former. In the grand hall he gave us a short lecture on the conferences held by James I, upon taking the throne, with the clergy and the puritans, each party hoping to gain his support. Old history becomes new when told in the very rooms whose walls witnessed and heard the facts narrated. After a long look through the gallaries and paintings and tapestry, and a walk through the beautiful grounds, we sat down to a superb luncheon in a tent in Bushy Park. This over, we took a most romantic walk to Teddington, about one mile, through an avenue of horse chestnuts. The trees are old and large. They stand twenty-five feet apart each way, and are seven rows deep on either side of the roadway. The gentleman in charge said that when they were in full blossom it was one of the sights of England, as we could well understand. The Cambridge party spoke enthusiastically of their trip and reception.

On Monday, in the recess, the principal librarian and keepers of the British Museum received the delegates at eleven o'clock and conducted them through that famous building, especially exhibiting the original records of the Westminster Assembly. On Wednesday at four o'clock, Dean Bradley of Westminster Abbey received the delegates in the Nave and conducted them into the famous Jerusalem chambers, where the work of revising the scriptures was carried on. Lord Balfour took a party of fifty over the House of Lords. Admission was also furnished to the Commons. This is not so easily obtained now as before the attempts at destruction by dynamite there and in the Tower. An omnibus ride to Bunhill Fields was also offered. There lie the remains of John Bunyan and De Foe, whose writings are household words. The Bible Society gave a reception also, and the Tract Society made a present to each delegate of the bound volumes of their works. Thus the endeavor was made to show hospitality equal to the best, and we think the effort was crowned with success.

The second day the council met in Exeter Hall, where the sessions were held to the end. The lower hall was occupied, but in a very short time the meeting was crowded out into the great hall above, where it continued. A fine attendance of visitors was maintained throughout in the day, while the evening sessions, of a more popular character, were densely thronged. Stretched across the end of the building, completely covering the great organ, still hung the map of the world in use by the missionary conference, whose meetings have but just now ended. By the by, it is a singular comment on the fact, that journals closely follow the trend of public demand in the matter of news, that although I have not been out of the British Isles during the sittings of that body, I have not been able to find ten lines of news from it, while reading the papers daily. You know in America, west end, ten times as much as I do here in England of what happened there. I am told that certain papers made a specialty of the conference, but I did not get hold of them ; and Dr. Ellingwood remarked in the closing meeting that it was singular that so much space could be given to a horse race or to a reception and none to the great matters of sending the gospel to the ends of the earth.

The papers presented and subjects discussed covered a wide range of questions that are considered vital as well as those of a practical nature. The great points reached after in all were truth and efficiency, truth as the solid foundation and efficiency in application. The first day's discussions were devoted to the practical working of the eldership and to church worship. In the latter case the methods in vogue in our western world were soundly condemned in general principle. In making the application for myself I certainly could not defend some of the western methods, either from scripture or from the fruit they bear in actual experience. The next day was devoted to intellectual difficulties and scientific hinderances to faith, and how to deal with them most effectively. This was a warm day inside, as may be supposed. In smooth language, and with gentle intonation, papers were read that set all to thinking most profoundly, and some to raising objections and offering criticisms. Very advanced ideas were set forth and received kindly, and shot through and through by those who did not agree, and all was smiling and peaceful. It was the playing of lions, one could easily reason to their more determined struggles. Then came co-operation on foreign mission fields with testimony from missionaries from all parts of the world as to the evils of having so many bodies represented there. The entire sentiment was in favor of co-operation, and the council has advanced that idea very much by its action.

Woman's work in all its phases was discussed, with many a good word for these most faithful upholders of the Master's interests. Professor Charteris, of Edinburgh, opened it with a paper that was criticised much as to its exegesis of scripture touching the place of women in the public services of the church. The council heartily indorsed their work, and bade them God speed. All agreed that it marked the beginning of a new era in the church's aggressive work. Much attention was given to the Colonial and European churches, in which department lie many of those feeble ones whom this alliance is intended to benefit. They were made to feel that they were not by any means alone and without sympathy.

A very rich day was that given to the young. The children hold a very warm place in our hearts, a fact that was evidenced by the full attendance all day. It was my honor to have the main place in opening the subject in an address upon "More Advanced Ideas in America Upon Sunday School Matters." The appointment fell to me in the absence of Dr. Worden. The statement of our ideas and practices awakened great interest, and called for private inquiry afterwards on points. The council was not ready to accept all we think and do, but gladly made note of them for further consideration. Thus the seed is sown, and in far away lands it will bear fruit of which neither you nor I may ever hear. The grand thing is to have good methods, and then tell them out, because you know that they are good. The evening was filled up on these same topics by such men as Dr. Holmes, of Albany, New York; Dr. Hall, of New York, and Rev. Mr. Neil, the Spurgeon of Scotland, as he is called. Thus in a rough and hasty way I have given to you a nibble from the great feast.

The organization of the Alliance is more fully perfected by creating the office of chief secretary, at a salary of $2,500 per annum, and an American secretary without compensation. The first is to have no other occupation, and is to reside in Great Britain. Rev. Dr. Matthews, of Quebec, was elected chief secretary, and will remove to London on the first of October, at which time his salary will begin. Rev. Dr. Roberts, of Cincinnati, was chosen the American assistant. He will be invaluable to the American churches. This Alliance has, through the ignorance of the secretaries as to the caliber and fitness of the Americans, been largely Scotch in its papers and reports. No man can better correct this than the assistant secretary chosen, who is the stated clerk of the General Assembly of the Northern Church.

The Alliance gave very distinct utterance to the sentiments of the church on the question of the introduction of liquor into the Pacific Islands. Earl Granville states that in response to an official proposition that the various governments interested should join to prevent the selling of liquor and gunpowder, he had received favorable word from all but two, and one of these was the United States. It was a stinging rebuke to the American delegates, and made us blush for our nation. The quality of some of the liquor sold in the Congo Free States is such that it is in testimony by naturalists that it destroys instead of preserving natural history specimens. On all such questions the foremost nation should be on the right side, and we hope soon to see America there.

In its sessions the council made repeated mention in prayer of the great Pan Angelican Council of Bishops now in session in Lambeth Palace, seat of the Archbishop of Canterbury. A resolution was passed conveying to them formally our Christian regards and salutations. The great bodies of the religious world are drawing closer together. Some in cold disdain prefer as yet to stand aloof, but it is rapidly getting chilly out there. The evening of rank denominationalism is falling, and all will come in out of the damp and cold by and by, if not in organic union at least in effective co-operation. To this end the Alliance of Presbyterian Churches is ever progressing, both between the scattered members of her own family and between herself and all families of those who hold the true evangelical faith of the ever-living Word of God.

FRANCIS A. HORTON.

LETTER XIV.

GENEVA, July 20, 1888.

I wish to speak a good word for Scarborough, up in Yorkshire, England. I hurried you down to London, and my conscience has accused me ever since of having slighted a friend. This I never do; friendship is a sacred word with me, and the thing itself once killed is like the slaying of a person—the precious life is gone forever, beyond possibility of restoration. So to square up things with Scarborough I will tarry long enough to say that the people of York- shire may murder their h's to the amusement of the world, they may have a dialect of their own that needs interpretation to out- siders, but so long as they have York Minster for architecture, and Scarborough for seaside resort, they may·hold up their heads and expose their big, red, masculine faces to the gaze of the world with- out a blush. As Oliver Wendell Holmes prettily puts it in another connection, nature has been "throwing her red roses against their faces" so long that perhaps a blush might exist inwardly, yet find no place to appear outwardly. But up there on the coast of the North sea, just across from Holland, is one of nature's gems, and appreciative man has polished it into a thing of beauty. A deep bay, with coast line curving inward for many a league, then sweep- ing outward again; a high bluff, not less than five hundred feet above the sea, sloping down to right, to left, and gently falling toward the sea, with park upon the seaward declivity with paths winding down; a lovely beach covered with children playing in the sand, with dogs running madly into the breakers and out again, with ponies and donkeys saddled and ready for the mount, with bathing cars, with boats in endless variety and number almost, manned by weather-beaten seamen, whose visages bespeak knowl- edge of the sea and inspire the terra firma heart with confidence; a grand pavilion, with seats for hundreds, and a band discoursing sweetest music, a city embowered in trees, with shady walks on every hand, with deep glens ornamented in high art, with waterfall, and pond, and swimming ducks, and swans, bright vehicles and pleasing occupants, good hotels and comfortable lodgings—such is the panorama that will long roll and unroll itself before my mind as I think of Scarborough. Brighton is larger and more widely known, more expensive and fashionable, but to me it can never compare with the little cove in Yorkshire.

Speaking of dialect, I am reminded of a man and wife, most agreeable and pleasing to recall, with whom we traveled for some miles. She remarked that the Queen "was a decent woman." Seeing that we regarded that sage observation as a doubtful compliment, she explained by saying, "In Yorkshire 'decent' means a great deal. When you want to say the best you can of a person just call him 'decent.'" After winding about in York, which is as interesting itself to me as is the Minster, turning in and out of the narrow streets as fancy moved us, shopping here and pricing there, we found that our time had got away from us, and that we needed to make haste to get away after it. So I asked a citizen to show me a short cut out. He said, "Just go into yon snicket and push through." "Yon what?" said I. "Yon snicket where you see the open door." So we went to hunt the snicket, passed through an opening in the wall the size of an ordinary door, and found ourelves hemmed in between buildings so close together that in places we could touch them on both sides at once by extending the arms. It wound this way and that way, and all along were tenement houses with front doors opening upon the snicket, so that a sense of intrusion upon privacy naturally quickened our steps and suppressed our merriment at the strange adventure and experience. But in true Boston style the short cut put us out just where we wanted to be, and saved us many a step on crowded streets. I am not an expert philologist, but wife and I concluded that snicket must be a corruption of "sneak out."

The old Minster is getting to be more and more a burden of expense. In many places the stone is chipping off, and if one applies an unsanctified hand to the severed relic of a past age at such a place the sand will be found to have little cohesion, crumbling easily away under the pressure. I wonder, as I look about, whether stone ever gets the dry rot, and whether there may not come a day when in spite of care and expense these venerable old piles will come down. It seems as though the only positive assurance to the contrary is actual rebuilding stone by stone as weakness appears.

Now having done my duty to Yorkshire I shall bring you over the channel with me, remarking that your passage, on paper, will be

9

no more free from sea-sickness than was mine, and no less so. The
morning was beautiful, and the sea was tired out with a terrible
storm that had been raging for several days. So while it was resting and getting ready to do up some more voyagers, we slipped over
in peace and quiet.

Looking back upon Paris from this mountain city on the banks
of the bluish, greenish Rhone and the lovely lake that takes its
name, I wish to speak a good word for our hostess in that city,
which will be a good word also to any who may make a note
of it for future use. To many persons hotel life is unpleasant. I
sicken of it very soon. To others the expense is an item of much
importance. It always has been and probably always will be to me.
So the great mass of people like a hint here and there of a better
and a less costly way of getting on. For their sakes and to possess
their gratitude I mention my dear Madame Riston, 80 Avenue
Kleber, whose house is a home and an hotel combined, whose
kindness and thoughtfulness are unceasing and wonderfully agreeable in a strange city, in a foreign land. You take to her at once,
and keep on taking to her until you leave, and then want all in
whom you have any interest to take to her, too. For a score of
years she kept a young ladies' boarding school in New York, and so
is thoroughly acquainted with our ways, wherefore her house is very
popular with Americans. It contains some twenty-five rooms, so
there is almost always a possibility of being accommodated if notice
is given befo ehand. Her terms are ten francs per day, including
early and late breakfast and evening dinner, with room and attendance of course. Avenue Kleber is one of the twelve streets radiat-
ing from the Arc de Triomph, forming the "star." It is broad and
beautiful. No. 80 is about midway between the Arc and the Trocadero, not more than ten minutes' walk from either. Any one who
knows Paris will say that this is one of its very best quarters. And
as the exposition next year will center in the Trocadero and in the
Champs de Mars, the two being connected by a bridge across the
Seine, number 80 will have special value.

"You may take all the musty old castles and tumble down
churches and the like and I will take Paris," said my other self as
we were walking leisurely down one of the gorgeous streets in the
cool of the day. First, a broad sidewalk lined inside the curb with
a row of beautiful shade trees, then a wide, smoothly paved road-

way extending to a second curbing, then another row of trees, then a wide, graveled walk and a third row of trees, then an equestrian way and a fourth row of trees, then a second paved roadway and a fifth row of trees, and finally a second sidewalk, while over the fences on both sides gardens with shrubbery separate the houses from the avenue. No doubt Paris is the most beautiful city in the world. It has, however, two sides—cleanest and dirtiest, attractive and repulsive—both sets of description belong to it. The transient visitor endeavors, as far as may be, to overlook the latter, and the native is so accustomed to them that he never thinks of them. So all think and speak of its beauties and charms, and there is no end to the theme. Her galleries are studded with gems. One Madonna in the Luxembourg, with a dead boy at her feet and its weeping mother kneeling beside her with elbows in her lap and hands over her face, while the Madonna's eyes are raised heavenward, is a wonderful production. To look upon her is to pray, to hope, to feel a new inspiration; her face is a sermon, a heaven of rest, once seen is never to be forgotten, a presence ever abiding, an uplift ever felt. And this is but one, yet to me the divinest, the most deeply spiritual anywhere to be found. By the way, when you go to London do not fail to visit the Dore Gallery. That weird creature whose sign manual in our memories is for the most part snakes and billows of flame and writhing humanity, has given in this gallery some of the best conceptions of Jesus and his love extant. I think that no more ravishingly beautiful face of the Son of man is to be found than that of Dore's Christ coming down the steps of the Prætorium after conviction. His conception of Christ saying "Come unto me all ye that labor," etc., is also wonderful—one feels that it is exactly true. Yet in the Louvre there are some inexpressible faces of Jesus; they hold one tenderly, firmly, and appeal to the inmost soul. I do not like Peter Paul Rubens. I suppose it is artistic heresy to say so, but there, it is written down! and now bring on the thumbscrews and the rack. Nevertheless, I may say that having seen those gentle persuaders in the Tower of London, I wish it distinctly understood that I mean bring them on figuratively. I never saw the Rubens yet, I never entertained an opinion on art yet, for which I would stand long in the presence of those hideous arguments. I even wonder what kind of martyr timber there is in me. But at this safe distance in time and space I repeat I do not like

Rubens. He twists and distorts his figures, I suppose to show his wonderful knowledge of human anatomy, but the effect is extremely disagreeable. David is simply glorious. His paintings in the one room at Versailles, showing the end of human glory in the case of Napoleon, are enough of honorable achievement for one man. There we see Napoleon as boy, as man; Napoleon crowning Josephine; Napoleon giving the eagles to the army; and finally, in the center of the room, amid these grand portrayals of a life full of ambition and accomplishment, stands a marble statue showing the great general dying at St. Helena. Who can walk through these miles of paintings and not be the better for it? Would that we could visit them often, when the brain is weary and the pressure of care is heavy; when friends fall off and death seems a far more agreeable companion than men are wont to think; when thought is feeble and expression difficult; when we just hate books for we are overfull of them; then to walk silently here and look into face after face that seem to open a vista, stretching away into undreamed-of depths, to feel the impress of a presence that soothes as a mother, that instructs as a teacher, that administers as a doctor; to go on looking into deeper grief than you have ever known, into more hopeless friendliness than you have ever experienced; this, all this, is a soul bath in the best thought of the ages, in the holiest conceptions of humanity, and as a resultant to go out with burdens lifted, with courage renewed, this were invaluable. I have heard slightingly of marble tears, but if any human being ever wept warmer tears, or tears that touched more deeply the sympathy of the beholder than one marble woman is weeping in the Luxembourg, it has not been made known to man. O Art, thou art divine, and divinely canst thou bless us when portraying the love of God, the Infinite, and the love of man to fellow man! But while drifting naturally to the galleries when speaking of the charms of that fair, frail city, they are not all there by any means. Her churches are worthy of high mention, her public buildings, her parks, her monuments, all claim admiration. In one word, everybody who has anything to do in the way of improvement endeavors not only to see how it may be made to serve a useful end, but also how he may combine the beautiful with it.

The fourteenth of July was a great day. Everything yielded to the festive idea. A review of troops and a display of fireworks were the main features of a general public character, but the people, in their own way, sought amusement. Every cafe, and very many buildings, were decorated with the three-barred flag, and many also with the stars and stripes. Festoons were abundant, hung with Chinese lanterns. Wine flowed in rivers—men, women, and children using it without stint. The boys and girls, and children just able to toddle, feasted on bread and wine as if it were with us bread and milk. The wine was Bordeaux in many instances under my observation, a light drink, and as harmless as any wine can ever be. In the early part of the day, down in the lower part of the town along the Place Vendome and Rue de Rivoli, I saw, perhaps, a half dozen men who evidently had been drinking to excess, perhaps of absinthe, or some heavy liquor, quantities of which are used here. But after this I saw no one intoxicated nor boisterous. I was in the crowd all day, and at night in so dense a crowd that I was somewhat nervous and I give the facts simply. It is estimated that not less than one million of people were on the streets in the pursuit of pleasure on this day. Every tramcar and omnibus, and every steamer on the Seine, was crowded to the full limit of the law. Nothing so notable as the crowd itself, and its behavior, came under my eye. I saw no fighting; there was no pushing nor any rudeness; but as Madam said before I went out so I found it true, "You will find the French people very orderly and considerate." In the evening the new and useless iron tower, that is to be one thousand feet high and is now four hundred and fifty, was utilized for the display of fireworks. The Trocadero was illuminated gorgeously, the fountains playing under the gaslights, waterfalls pouring over with gaslight shining through—a picture of oriental splendor. The grounds of the Trocadero, from the steps of the building to the Seine, were one dense mass of human beings, while avenue Kleber was studded with carriages. Yet in all this moving mass of people, tired with standing after a long day of festivity, impatient at the delay of the exhibition, not one loud voice, not one angry word was heard. To me it was a remarkable fact. A real live Irishman, after picnicing in his accustomed way, would have been heard from a dozen times in the same period. Another fact was the absence of policemen—at least they were not seen. Inside the gardens of the Trocadero they were pacing up and down to keep the crowd from attempting to invade them, but none were outside. I found no argument on all this.   Personally, I do not like their wine-drinking customs.   I do not uphold them ; I should deplore such a condition of things in America.   But so much has been said upon this subject that I set out to see for myself, and I have seen, and do testify that with wine flowing on every side, and consumed by old and young, fat and lean, nervous and sanguine, male and female, weak and strong, patrician and plebian, the state of things in public at eleven o'clock at night was as I have stated.   Yet a thousand times rather our home sentiment on this subject than the prevailing custom here.   It seems to me such a debasing practice, such a prostitution of the nobler to the lower nature, that while we cannot point to gutters filled with drunken people, somehow we feel that it is far below our level.   Somehow we are sure that it must, in the onflow of genera- tions, make its mark upon the health, the power, the permanence of the French republic.

Of the fireworks themselves, I will only say that they repaid all the trouble we were at to see them.   After they were over the crowd surged down the avenue.   I sat in my window and watched them pass for a long time, filling the street loosely from wall to wall.   I am told by others who prowled around later (for some people never can get enough), that there was dancing in every open place, while the Place de Concorde was ablaze with light, and merry dancers kept it up until towards morning.

The French horn wheezed and droned all day and far into the night.   Music has a soul, and any style of music that arrests and soothes the soul of the masses certainly interprets their inner expe- rience.   The French horn can be called nothing else than a cry of the soul in agony.   First one strikes in with a strain in minor key, then two or three more catch it up and all wail it out together. The bagpipe of Scotland is to me a most touching instrument when played by a skilled hand, and Scotch ballads are often painful.   At Roslyn an old man, with a voice of rare sweetness and pathos, stood before the inn, and accompanying himself on an accordion, sang Scotch songs.   The first verse hushed our talking, the second set us crying.   We were not feeling very happy at Edinburgh, and the old man struck the right chords in our hearts and soon did us up completely.   I wonder if the French soul is happy.   I do not see how it can be.   Its music says that it is not.   How different are our American songs and popular airs.   How different those of England.

France is prosperous. She wants peace, and will do anything in honor to preserve it. But is she secure? The deep religious convictions lying as corner-stones of our republic are wanting here to so great an extent that the future no man can determine.

FRANCIS A. HORTON.

LETTER XV.

STEAMER EIDER, NORTH GERMAN LLOYD, }
August 3, 1888. }

With a few additional notes of travel we will take leave of those kind friends who through the columns of *The Tribune* have camped and tramped with us for several months past. If they have taken a tithe of the pleasure therein that we have experienced in their company, our joy shall be full.

It was a gorgeous Sabbath morning when we awoke in Lucerne. To one who has stopped there for a day, or for a longer season, the mere mention of the name sends a thrill of pleasure through the soul, a warmth through the body, and the blood bounding through the veins. The beautiful, beatuiful water, the walks upon its banks, shaded by double and triple rows of sycamores topped in to make them spread and interlock their branches ; the life everywhere on land, on lake, in skiff, and yacht, and swift steamer, the glorious Alps rising beyond in long chains of snow-covered peaks, cooling the air, yet not cooling it, sending into it a delicious sense of freshness and vigor, while yet a sunshade is very acceptable, off there to the south the Rhigi, with its hotel perched in cloudland, a picture all that can never be effaced from the mind that has once taken it fully in, one that will be a joy to the soul so long as memory holds her seat. Then the bells ! Those Swiss bells—was anything ever sweeter? We talk of the church bell as a relic of barbarism. Let us not disgrace those ancient bells by suggesting that those which bang and clang in modern steeples have descended from them or are in any way related to them. These have a soul, and that soul has a song, and as they roll it and roll it out it reaches to our soul and sings its sweetness through all our being. One could hear them ring and sing for an hour, and forget them as they lift us up into loftier realms of thought, and soothe our cares and draw our tears until we feel that we have been holily wrought upon, if, indeed, we have not actually worshipped. If one not in the trade may venture a suggestion, we think that by attempting to cater to the idea of making less noise we have reduced the size of our bells until the music is all out of them and there is nothing left but a disagreeable residum of pure noise of the order of the Chinese gong. Then, too, the metal may have no tone in it because it is cheap, the attempt being to make a saleable bell. The church bell has a place, as any one will confess who has heard the bells of Lucerne, sending their voices over the waters to the distant hills beyond, yet so soothingly that the sick man near would be rested thereby, as a fevered child under the crooning of a nurse. With deep regret we turned our backs upon this charming spot, and with quickened pulse shall we come to the day, should it ever be ours, when we shall revisit it and tarry longer.

Dashing along the railway to Frankfort-on-Main, we saw the harvest in full blast. We could not but make a note of the part the woman takes in all of these hard manual labors. It filled our soul with pity, trained as we had been in a different system. The man, with his funny little cradle, cuts down the grain, and the woman stoops to earth, as though she had no back to ache, and gathers it together into bundles and binds it. She carries the bundles into heaps. She pitches them upon the load. She rakes down the loaded wagon, and rakes after the wagon, and this, not in one or two instances, but everywhere and all the way. In no country in the world does woman, not in favored classes, but woman as such, hold the place that she does in America. Just look over the rail here into the steerage and see the women sitting about. Look at those arms, bare, and brown, and brawny; look at those hands spread out of shape; at those thick fingers, those broad, hard, finger-nails, what evidences of toil in manual labor; how wearily the body sinks together, the shoulders stooping, the clasped hands presssed deeply into the lap; poor, tired mortal, we know what burdens you have borne, we are happy to think that every turn of the Eider's screw is sending you fifty feet nearer to a land where your daughter or granddaughter will come into a condition of which you have to-day, as you sit musing on that coil of rope, no faintest conception. In all these European lands it is the same. We find women carrying stone and mortar, attending upon workmen; we find them doing menial work, dragging carts, cleaning streets, and

the like. The difference is most noticeable in other ways. I think
I mentioned the remark of our accomplished young English board-
ing-house keeper in London. It will bear repeating. She said:
"What we English people notice most of all in our American guests
is the attention the married men show to their wives, the care they
take of them, and the way they wait upon them. With us it is
quite the reverse." As a result of our methods we may produce a
race of women, not so robust, not able to walk so many miles, raising fewer children, with more headache and backache, but take the
rank and file of them through, from the lowliest to the most exalted,
there is an airness, a freshness, a springing gait, an intelligence in
eye and word, and a delicacy and refinement that we look for in
vain elsewhere. We are not prejudiced, but simply stating observed
facts with balanced judgment.

Everybody speculates about German politics in these days—
except ourselves. But having the hearing ear and the recording
pencil we may be pardoned a reflection. There is undoubtedly a
large element in Germany that sympathizes with the late Emperor
Frederick in the belief that the taking of Alsace and Lorraine was
a mistake; that Germany did not need the territory and that that
act will certainly produce trouble in days to come. It is stated,
with some show of authority, that Frederick contemplated a bold
proposition in the way of a peaceful restoration. The present
Emperor, therefore, recently in saying with the heartlessness of a
Napolean that he would prefer to see his German corps cut to
pieces rather than restore one piece of acquired territory, or words
to that effect, was not beating a man of straw, it was aimed at this
sentiment that is freely expressed in the fatherland. A most intelligent German, while glorying in that acquisition on the ground of
national pride, as all do, admitted over the table d'hote in the very
hotel in Frankfort in one of the upper rooms of which the treaty of
Frankfort was prepared and signed, that trouble would yet come of
it. On the Freach side the immortelles are never wanting on the
statue representing Strasburg in the Place du Concorde in Paris,
and always French flags may be seen crossed upon it draped in
mourning. No one can forecast the future. The French people,
rank and file, are wearied with the Republic, they are ready for a
change.

The surprising success of Boulanger in the recent elections only
10

confirms the statement made to me by an intelligent resident in Paris one day, in the galleries of Versailles, that "the people were tired of the republic; they were far more miserable and poorly governed than under the empire." I confess I was surprised, and took the statement with mental reservations. But it seems to be nearer the truth after all. So there are wheels within wheels, currents and counter-currents, and what the outcome may be none can say.

Embarking at Mainz we sailed down the Rhine to Cologne. We did not find the Rhine so wonderful, and we did not find all of those odors at Cologne. The river is beautiful; the city is clean and pleasing. Comparisons are not pleasant. I only venture to say I am not dissatisfied that I was born on the banks of the Hudson. Nature, antiquity, and industry make up the charms of the river. Nature, in a copious stream, winding among hills of respectable size and height; antiquity, in crowning these otherwise uninteresting hills with castles that people the heights with imaginary men and armies and pass long reaches of history and romance before the mind; industry, that has constructed miles upon miles of stone terraces, from summit to water's edge, to make possible the cultivation of the grape on those steep sides. This is the Rhine, a river of which every German is properly proud, and on which every tourist may and should spend a very pleasant day. The wines raised on the shore are for sale on board, or are supposed to be. And the capacity of man and woman to contain those sour drinks is simply wonderful. Rudesheimer, Oppenheimer, and many other heimers follow each other down all day long, with no effect visible, save that they flush the ladies and blonde young men to the roots of the hair. When we went on board at Mainz, one man and two women had taken possession of one of the many tables on deck, and were drinking a white wine; after finishing this they called for some sandwiches and wine; this done they had a red wine, then came dinner, when they took a wine to assist digestion. We thought surely that they were done now, but lo! on ascending to the deck they met a few friends, and the group took a new table, and each of the male members ordered his favorite brand of wine, and finished as the high towers of the Cologne Cathedral appeared above the plains looming heavenward, while all other objects adjacent to it were still below the horizon of plain vision. It was the longest drink I had ever witnessed, and they seemed to regret the end. The statement has been made that only 2,000,000 gallons of wine consumption for California last year was truly lamentable ; that Paris would consume it in two days. May a kind Providence long defend us against such guzzling, such senseless, sottish, extravagant consumption of harmless wines as one sees in Paris and on the Rhine. Everything has its place ; we do not deny it to the mild wines of the old world where any find their moderate use medicinal, as so many claim. But if that admission is in any way likely to bring in its train such drinking for the mere sake of killing time, or for seeing how much one can hold, or worse, from national habit, until only the fact of the excess is apparent to a stranger visitor, then say I, perish every vine in California, welcome blizzards to blight, phylloxera to destroy. Yes, perish the vines and save the people. This excessive use must work great and detrimental changes in national tone, and temper, and constitution in long years. The first effect, we learn, is a sense of weariness inducing sleep. But says my apologist, a young lady, this is the thing desired ; we Americans work too hard, we come here to rest, and we want to sleep. The next effect is when the brain is struggling up from this stupidity and finds itself fettered, then comes irritability, and the French wine-drinker is on fire in a moment. Those terrible welts on his horse's side, those blood-oozing blows, may have come straight from his light wine-cup. Continue this, day after day, and year after year, and a permanent deterioration of character must ensue. Spare America a practically free wine bottle.

At last in Bremerhafen our eyes fell upon the good ship Eider, in which we were to go down upon the deep once more for the voyage home. The ladies thought she looked small to be charged with so important a responsibility, but she was distant, and behind her was a background of ocean that made her look smaller by comparison. We found her an admirable craft, costing about $1,000,000 ; her saloon and smoking-room alone costing £40,000 for fittings, including paintings, etc. The rooms are large, ventilation is good, everything is clean and orderly, the officers are gentlemen off duty, and unapproachable when on duty, especially when the weather is at all thick ; the tables are supplied bountifully, ice cream, for example, being carried from New York in quantity to be served to the saloon passengers every day at dinner, out and return, and to second cabin three times a week on outward and homeward voyages. It is packed in small paper boxes and then put in refrigerators, like Washington hokey-pokey. The stewards of the second cabin are hired with reference to their musical ability as well as to their proficiency as waiters. They form a band, and are supplied with excellent instruments, wind and string. They play as a band on deck and as an orchestra in the saloon while the first cabin is at dinner. Their dinner programme consists of six well chosen pieces, varying from popular airs up to high opera. When soup is ready the music strikes up and the waiters file in, the music continuing through all the courses, responses being made to encores cheerfully. The pleasure herein is very great, and the profit, too, for this mental diversion to some small extent counteracts sea-sickness and enables a person to remain at table who otherwise would go climbing up the rubber stairs to the deck. Good speed is attained every day, not far from four hundred miles either way. Take it for all in all, it is one of the pleasantest lines on the ocean. But my creed for ocean travel has only one article, viz.: we believe in the swiftest ships consistent with safety and the shortest distance between getting on and off.

Bishop Doane, of Albany, was one of our number, and a genial companion, as well as a most learned churchman. He was returning from the Lambeth Convocation, and complained of being preached almost to death. He gave us a good discourse on the lesson for the second Sabbath of our voyage.

We had a little sensation which might have filled a few columns of a morning daily were it not that a miss is as good as a mile. The horrible fog had closed us in for a couple of days, during which the depressing signal had been blowing at regular intervals, making us dread to go down below, and afraid to fall asleep. But we did fall off, until we were awakened by the stillness. One becomes so accustomed to the regular beating of the great engine's pulse that when it ceased it awakened us. We listened for the screw and could not hear it, yet felt a slight tremor, showing that we were moving enough to keep steerage way. Then came an answer to our fog horn out of the white wet blanket around us—call and answer, call and answer—then suddenly as though the ship were leaping back from a yawning chasm came an awful shaking. It was the screw reversing at full speed—we were backing away from something. Out of berth we flew, and with head out of porthole peered into the fog. As good luck would have it, we were on the port side, and were just in time to see a three-masted schooner with sails set falling across our bow from the starboard side. In another instant the fog closed her in, and we could hear her horn for a little time only. It was a close call for one or the other of us. Had we struck her there would have been two of her in a trice ; had she struck us, we, personally, might have got out of our room alive, as we were on the port side, but I have no idea that this letter would ever have been written. The chances of being saved, in such an event, are so slim that it is a wonder any one ever lives to tell the tale. But we came safely through, and presume that in due course of years we may brave the fogs again.

At last came the pilot, full five hundred miles out at sea and with him papers from home several days old, but still new to us. Then in due course the lights along the shore began to appear and finally the warm breath of an American August and the genial welcome of the industrious mosquito. Our hearts arose with the rising shore lines and the mountain steeples, and our palates began to clamor for green corn, and butter with salt in it.

After all, how much of life is made up of little things, and how little a thing life is itself. Yet happiness is in attention to little things, and if, in noting with some detail the little haps and mishaps of our most enjoyable wandering, we have prepared any intending tourist the better for his outing, we shall feel as amply rewarded as though we had brought great things to those who through carefully written books of travel have had a surfeit of them already.

FRANCIS A. HORTON.

I I